The Printed Prophets

To order additional copies of *The Printed Prophets,*
by Lemuel Olán Jiménez, **call 1-800-765-6955.**

Visit us at **www.reviewandherald.com** for information on other
Review and Herald® products.

The Printed Prophets

The Vital Role of Literature in the Last Days

Lemuel Olán Jiménez

REVIEW AND HERALD® PUBLISHING ASSOCIATION

Since 1861 | www.reviewandherald.com

Published by Review and Herald® Publishing Association, Hagerstown, MD 21741-1119

This book was
Edited by Gerald Wheeler
Copyedited by Amy Prindle
Cover designed by Daniel Anéz / Review and Herald® Design Center
Cover art by Thinkstock
Interior designed by Emily Ford / Review and Herald® Design Center
Typeset: 11/13 Minion Pro

PRINTED IN U.S.A.

17 16 15 14 13   5 4 3 2 1

Library of Congress Cataloging-in-Publication Data
Jiménez, Lemuel Olán.
   The printed prophets : the vital role of literature in the last days / by Lemuel Olán Jiménez.
      pages cm
   1. Christian literature—Publishing. 2. Missions. 3. End of the world. 4. Seventh-day Adventists—Doctrines. I. Title.
   BR44.J56 2013
   230'.6732—dc23
                    2012049612
   ISBN 978-0-8280-2703-8

Dedication

To my loving wife, Martitha,
and to my children,
Lemuel Roberto, Esther Daniela, and Martha Alejandra,
and in memory of
Ord O. Kyte, visionary, man of God,
without whose selfless dedication I would not be a minister of the gospel.

Acknowledgments

I wish above all to thank our Sovereign Lord for the publication of this book. As Ellen G. White once said: "Often our plans fail that God's plans for us may succeed" (*Maranatha* [Washington, D.C.: Review and Herald Pub. Assn., 1976,] p. 321). It is exactly what has happened in the publication of this book. In loving patience the Lord's hand has guided in the development of its every section.

I also wish to thank Pastor José Luis Campos, who, as publishing ministries director for the General Conference, motivated me to continue researching when he heard the first embryonic ideas that later turned into the concepts presented here. His unselfish interest was a great inspiration to me. Now happily retired, he was generous enough to pen the foreword. Many thanks to him!

I am also privileged to mention Pastor Noé Alpirez Galindo, publishing ministries director for the North Mexican Union of the General Conference's Inter-American Division, for his constant prayers over this project. His lifelong dream of opening the heart of every church member to the importance of literature distribution has been a constant fountain of inspiration to me.

In a special way I wish to thank Pastor Esteban Griguol, publishing ministries director for the North American Division's Texas Conference. His enthusiasm proved to be a driving force that led to the timely completion of this project. In language known to literature evangelists everywhere I can confidently state that Pastor Griguol made the "final close" so that this book could at last see the light of day.

In the same breath I want to thank Pastor Luis Biazotto, director of the Review and Herald Publishing Association's Home Health Education Service, from the bottom of my heart. His team and facilities made publication possible. May God's grace in you translate into souls won through the ministry of the printed page. The Lord's coming is at the door!

Also deserving thanks are Manuel Médina, for providing valuable resources, and Caleb Torres Agúndez, for translating the manuscript from Spanish to English. Truly this has been a team effort.

Finally I thank my parents for their encouraging counsel at every step that led to the publication of this work, and for their loving interest in the message it contains. Their prayers turned into blessings that upheld my arms and hands as I continued writing.

May God bless you all.

Contents

Foreword

Written by a man passionate for the work of evangelism, using the method devised and used by God for centuries of human history, and in recent times confirmed through His messenger Ellen G. White, *The Printed Prophets* shows that the books printed by our publishing houses are preparing people for "the sealing" that the Angel of the Lord is carrying forward in our time. Lemuel Olán Jiménez seeks to awaken every member of our church, whether layperson or minister, to carry on and promote the mission that God in His mercy is waiting for us to complete.

The Printed Prophets deserves careful consideration on our part. Its seven chapters lead us to a healthy spiritual understanding of those biblical truths that highlight the importance of the literature ministry for our time and its even greater relevance to the days just ahead.

Despite the fact that we live in an age in which electronic devices and mass media seem to overshadow printed material, this book shows in well-documented fashion the importance of just this method in meeting the needs of a world facing its last great crisis, one that will severely challenge the effectiveness of other forms of evangelism.

Jiménez reveals that our church members, as they distribute lit–erature, are fulfilling a prophetic mission, as is the message of the literature they handle. He reassures us that in the final, rapid events of the approaching last days, Seventh-day Adventist literature will harvest abundant fruit for God's kingdom. Books and magazines containing transformative truths await the day that many children of God, eager to learn the truth, will find in them the seed that will sprout in their souls to everlasting life.

May it be God's will that *The Printed Prophets* finds its way into every church member's hand and that, whether layperson, minister, or leader, they will allow its vitalizing, visionary, and revealing message to redefine their participation in one of the greatest endeavors God designates His people to undertake in this time. May we each, as we play our roles, lift our eyes longingly at the thought that our Lord, whom we all love and long to see, is coming very soon in the clouds of heaven.

—Pastor José Luis Campos
   Publishing Ministries Department Director, 2000-2005
   General Conference of Seventh-day Adventists

Introduction

We live in solemn, awe-instilling times. The second coming of the Lord is at the door, and the signs of His approach are increasingly evident. Without a doubt we are on the cusp of events that will overwhelm the whole world in the immediate future. And yet we must bear in mind that *the Lord will appear only after the gospel message has been fully preached to the whole world* (Matt. 24:14). As such, we must awaken to the seriousness of the mission He has entrusted to us. We have special truths that we have yet to communicate to the vast majority of earth's teeming multitudes.

Mark Finley rightly reminds us that among our efforts toward revival, we must continually renew our commitment to save the lost:

"Why would God pour out His Spirit in latter rain power to finish His work if the majority of the church has little or no interest in witnessing? If the latter rain, the fullness of the Holy Spirit's power, is to empower the church to reach the world with God's end-time message, why would God give us the latter rain if we have a complacent, lukewarm attitude toward reaching lost people? The fullness of the Holy Spirit's power will be poured out on a praying, totally committed, unified, witnessing church."[1]

But is it really possible to make our message known and understood to an entire world? Recently I encountered a most audacious argument proposing that it is indeed possible to finish evangelizing the world simply by publishing books in the 10 most widely used world languages.[2] At first I found it difficult to take seriously, given that, according to another source,[3] more than 700 plans to evangelize the entire world have been proposed and none of them have succeeded in finishing the task (though admittedly, incredible advances in communications technology have greatly facilitated it).

While any claim that we can complete the task of evangelizing the world through literature alone is only to call attention to the impact generated by harnessing its power in massive numbers, sobering realities still demand that we must also employ other media. For example, about 793 million illiterate people live even in today's interconnected world.[4] Clearly the task may not be so simple after all.

Despite these facts, some hardworking Christians give publishing a very prominent role. In his push to reach the whole world an Assemblies of God leader recently said:

"Christian literature anointed by the Holy Spirit is always effective, and the only way, I believe, that we will be able to fulfill Christ's injunction to reach all the world."[5]

His most recent goal is to distribute 92.5 million books. Using a well-defined plan, his group has so far distributed more than 800 million copies[6] of *The Book of Hope* in various countries around the world.

George Verwer has also stated that only through the printed page will we ever fulfill the enormous task of leaving the gospel in every home on the planet, and he insists that many others share his belief.[7] And it does not obviate the use of other media.

Another mass-literature plan is Every Home for Christ, a systematic distribution of evangelical literature to every home in various countries in cooperation with local churches and missionaries.[8] It has so far circulated 3.25 billion pieces of literature. Dick Eastman, one of the program leaders, states on the cover of his book: "A global movement is under way to reach every home for Christ. The impact will be . . . beyond imagination."[9]

Clearly such leaders see publishing playing a decisive role in the completion of the preaching of the gospel. Yet they were far from the first to reach such a conclusion. Martin Luther once said that the press is "God's highest and extremest act of grace, whereby the business of the gospel is driven forward."[10]

But Luther's statement makes the most sense in the context of the sixteenth century, when no other media capable of reaching the masses existed. Does not broadcast media today enjoy greater popularity than print media? Our time has seen the advent of radio, television, and the now-ubiquitous explosion of online content. So why revisit the printed page? Aren't we currently witnessing the transformation of print media into an electronic form?

We can be forgiven for falling prey to the claim that literature just doesn't have the pull it had in past ages and that although important, it surely doesn't come in third, fourth, or even fifth place in use and prominence—or is there something about the printed page that we haven't yet realized? You may be surprised to learn that in the context of the last great crisis, print media will be one of the most crucial means that the Lord will use to save millions from the deadly delusions looming in the future.

Together we will examine why silent preaching—through our books, magazines, and pamphlets—is perfectly adapted to our time and why it will have such relevance in the rapid diffusion of the gospel at the very end. Ellen White observes that "it is as good and successful a method as can be employed for placing before the people the important truths for this time."[11] In another place we find a statement that, when read closely, finds its context in the very final days:

"In a large degree through our publishing houses is to be accomplished the work of that other angel who comes down from heaven with great power, and who lightens the earth with his glory."[12]

As a church we have not been unmindful of the inspired counsel:

"The book work should be the means of quickly giving the sacred light of present truth to the world."[13]

Several years ago the General Conference launched "Tell the World Until All Have Heard," an effort to distribute millions of books around the world[14] with the aim of involving every baptized member of the church. Alejandro Bullón recently wrote *Signs of Hope* for the program. And most recently *The Great Hope* has become the world church's largest-ever sharing book thrust.

We know that God wants to do something big in our time and that publications will constitute one of His key instruments. Thus the church's efforts to use this means is as never before. For example, on Sabbath, March 24, 2012, the church in South America distributed 25 million copies of *The Great Hope,* a condensed version of *The Great Controversy,* in a single day![15] Surely it is a sign that God is waking up His church to finish the task of preaching the gospel over the whole earth.

Please consider what this means. The final stretch of the finishing of the gospel is now under way. The fact remains that we can still consider publications as one of the most important means of fulfilling the church's mission.

In the first chapter, "Prophets of the Coming Crisis,"[16] we examine the following: In spite of our corporate dependence on mass media to proclaim the gospel, at the end of the day the primitive church blueprint calls for the active participation of every single church member. Therefore we will analyze the challenges that will await us when end-time events curtail satellite evangelism, then encourage the reader to reconsider the place of literature in the context of the fast-approaching final crisis.

The second chapter, "Silent Preachers in the Eye of the Storm," studies our time in the light of Revelation 7, then focuses our attention on the

Lord's soon return and what we as a church should be doing to hasten His coming.

The third chapter, "Prophets of the Final Sealing," reveals which prophecy this silent work fulfills and launches the challenge of becoming a part of this prophetic movement.

The fourth chapter explores how our literature is like "Prophets That Speak in the Wilderness," who will proclaim with extraordinary power once the latter rain of the Holy Spirit is poured out, and how it will explode into prominence when we reach the end.

The fifth chapter, "Prophets That Burn but Are Not Consumed," explains why society bans and burns books and shows that despite numerous attempts to eradicate them, such silent messengers will continue proclaiming their message until the end of probation.

The sixth chapter, "Prophets That Save Multitudes," brings out the redemptive objectives of the biblical message and its use and reminds us that the "great multitude" (understood as synonymous with the 144,000) is the long-term mission of the church.

Finally, "Prophets Proclaiming All Around You" describes the ways each church member must cooperate with the print messengers in the greatest work the Bible predicts will happen in our time: *the finishing of the proclamation of the gospel through myriad byways globally, everywhere and wherever humanity dwells* (Rev. 14:6; Matt. 24:14).

Without a doubt the owner of the vineyard is hastening to reap the harvest, and each and every church member, whatever their responsibility, will receive as great a reward as the men in the parable (see Matt. 20:6, 9, 12). The reader will learn how to work in harmony with the owner of the vineyard and share His sense of urgency. It is a ministry in which each can participate:

"When church members realize the importance of the circulation of our literature, they will devote more time to this work."[17]

It is my prayer that "the word of the Lord may have free course, and be glorified" (2 Thess. 3:1). Truly there is nothing near as relevant for the times we are living in. With Dick Eastman we can say, "The impact will be beyond anyone's imagination."

---

[1] Mark Finley, *Revive Us Again* (Boise, Idaho: Pacific Press Pub. Assn., 2010), p. 124.
[2] Bob Hoskins, *How to Hasten the Second Coming* (Deersfield, Fla.: Editorial Vida, 1992), p. 98.

[3] David B. Barrett, James W. Reapsome, *Seven Hundred Plans to Evangelize the World: The Rise of a Global Evangelization Movement* (Birmingham, Ala.: New Hope, 1988), p. 13.

[4] www.unesco.org/new/en/media-services/single-view/news/8_september_international_literacy_day_793_million_adults_can_neither_read_nor_write/. Accessed March 22, 2012.

[5] Bob Hoskins, *All They Want Is the Truth* (Miami: Life Publishers, 1985), pp. 104, 105.

[6] "One Hope. God's Word. Every Child," www.onehope.net. Accessed January 30, 2012.

[7] George Verwer, *Literature Evangelism* (Waynesboro, Ga.: OM Publishing, 2003), p. 1.

[8] www.ehc.org/about-us-vision-mission.

[9] www.ehc.org/about-us-history; Dick Eastman, *Beyond Imagination: A Simple Plan to Save the World* (Grand Rapids: Chosen Books, 1997).

[10] Elizabeth L. Eisenstein, *The Printing Revolution in Early Modern Europe* (New York: Cambridge Univ. Press, 2005), p. 165.

[11] Ellen G. White, *Colporteur Ministry* (Mountain View, Calif.: Pacific Press Pub. Assn., 1953), p. 6.

[12] Ellen G. White, *Christian Service* (Washington, D.C.: Review and Herald Pub. Assn., 1925), p. 148.

[13] E. G. White, *Colporteur Ministry*, p. 3.

[14] Matthew Bediako, "Tell the World, Until All Have Heard," *Adventist Review*, June 27, 2010.

[15] http://greatcontroversyproject.adventist.org.

[16] This book will use the term *prophet* to mean someone or something that is in the place of God to communicate a message. *Prophet* refers to "someone who first received instruction from the Lord and then conveyed it to the people. These two aspects of the prophet's work were reflected in the names by which prophets were known in Old Testament times: seer (*chozeh* or *ro'eh*) and prophet (*nabi'*). The title of seer was more common in the earlier period of Hebrew history (1 Sam. 9:9). The term used more frequently in the Old Testament was *nabi'*, "prophet," which designated him as God's spokesman. As a "seer" the prophet discerned God's will, and as "prophet" he conveyed it to others" (*Seventh-day Adventist Bible Dictionary* [Washington, D.C.: Review and Herald Pub. Assn., 1960, 1979], p. 903). The Bible not only calls the two witnesses of the written message the Old and New Testament (Rev. 11:3) prophets but also employs the term to refer to the people of God whose mission is to prophesy in the time of the end (Rev. 10:11). As a result we refer to our written message as a prophet in the sense that it can accomplish the mission of the church: communicating God's message of salvation to the whole world.

[17] E. G. White, *Colporteur Ministry*, p. 7.

Chapter 1

Prophets of the Coming Crisis

What kind of difficulties, challenges, and opportunities do we face in finishing the preaching of the gospel? As you read this book you will see that every living Seventh-day Adventist man, woman, and child is standing before an opportunity that has never before been encountered by any other generation. Though each will face awesome challenges in the drive to share the last gospel message, each of us also has the incredible potential of being instrumental in the transformation of vast groups of people, wherever we happen to live in the world—and all this through stunningly simple means. Are you interested?

"The present is a time of overwhelming interest to all living," wrote Ellen G. White. "Rulers and statesmen, men who occupy positions of trust and authority, . . . have their attention fixed upon the events taking place about us. . . . They observe the intensity that is taking possession of every earthly element, and they recognize that something great and decisive is about to take place—that the world is on the verge of a stupendous crisis." Then she adds that, at this very moment, "a storm is gathering," its malevolent fury "ready to burst upon the earth."[1]

If she wrote that more than a century ago, how much closer are we to seeing its predicted fulfillment? Much closer than we care to imagine, partly out of the self-awareness that it will be a time of intense difficulty for the church! The dragon will make one last effort to destroy God's people (Rev. 12:17). How will the church, facing such unpleasant odds, make headway with truths that so many will regard as the height of heresy? And who would voluntarily champion such a controversial cause?

"The work which the church has failed to do in a time of peace and prosperity she will have to do in a terrible crisis under most discouraging, *forbidding* circumstances."[2]

The world, experiencing the death throes of Satan's last desperate struggle, will blame God's people for its troubles:

"And then the great deceiver will persuade men that those who serve God are causing these evils."[3]

Circumstances will reach such a fever pitch that even before the authorities pronounce a death decree against them, they will regard the faithful as deserving of "universal execration."[4] How will such conditions affect God's people? And what exactly did Ellen White mean by "forbidding"?

Let's define some terms before continuing. First, the missionary strength of the church rests within every single church member, independent of place or position. That will be especially true in the final struggle:

"Servants of God, with their faces lighted up and shining with holy consecration, will hasten from place to place to proclaim the message from heaven. By thousands of voices, all over the earth, the warning will be given."[5]

It means that the full, final responsibility for the preaching of the gospel both now and in the future lies with the members of the church.

Second, I want to emphasize that God will call into action agencies currently known only to Him to aid in completing the vast task:

"When divine power is combined *with human effort,* the work will spread like fire in the stubble. *God will employ agencies whose origin man will be unable to discern;* angels will do a work which men might have had the blessing of accomplishing had they not neglected to answer the claims of God."[6]

Stated another way, this passage declares that God will finish His mission through those who are faithful to duty and that He will crown their efforts with success.

In the same breath I wish to make clear that I have nothing against mass broadcast media as currently used by the church to push ahead its divine commission. Nor is any one method of delivery single-handedly superior to another. Broadcast media serve a unique function: They afford the church a way to cast a wide net and "catch" many who might otherwise take no notice of the tidings of the third angel. It would in fact be a fatal blunder to argue that only individuals with a few lines and hooks should fish the wide ocean of people when vast schools of fish wait to be netted. Yet as one Sabbath school quarterly noted in its introduction, even when we harness all the benefits of modern broadcast media it is a classic understatement to say that the effort is still an overwhelming task.[7]

Too many of us fall prey to the happy fantasy of believing that satellite television, radio, and Internet evangelism are the sum total of public evangelism. Some favor radio, others television, and still others online outreach. In this book I will argue that all distributable literature bearing the third angel's message plays a central role in the diffusion of our story today and will assume an even larger one in the immediate future. Stated simply, broadcast media, despite their present glory, will not have the accessibility in the coming struggle that a simple book has and always will have.

It is my conclusion that in the context of the repressive environments predicted to take hold everywhere, the printed page will play a key role in delivering our message. But I want to highlight the relevance of sharing the message now, especially through books and other print media, for reasons that I will develop as we move through each chapter.

For now, is it possible to define more thoroughly the word "forbidding" that Ellen White used in the above quote? In the wealth of messages we have from her concerning the final struggle, it is not difficult to conclude that our broadcast media outlets will one day be censored or entirely banned by governments around the world.

"Sometimes it is important to control the flow of information," say some experts, "particularly where the situation pertains to religious problems and information wrongly distributed in a tense situation can cause explosive results."[8]

We find much included in John's statement in Revelation that the dragon will mount a last desperate struggle against those who "keep the commandments of God, and have the testimony of Jesus Christ" (Rev. 12:17).

Media censorship is nothing new. It has existed since the dawn of recorded human history and should therefore surprise no one. As we are now seeing in the world of online media, it can happen anywhere, unexpectedly, with little input from the public. Experts point out that "numerous governments censor the media for political, security, and moral reasons, as well as others." And Ellen White leaves this reminder:

"Those who honor the Bible Sabbath will be denounced as enemies of law and order, as breaking down the moral restraints of society, causing anarchy and corruption. . . . They will be accused of disaffection toward the government."[9] All this will produce "perplexities that are scarcely dreamed of."[10]

The enemies of the gospel will attempt to block all manner of potential avenues through which our message could find its way to people. The mass media will falter because they "have always been the captive of religion and politics, scorned and manipulated by both in ways beyond anything suffered by book publishers."[11] Even beyond that, the question of faithful Seventh-day Adventists making large media purchases in a no-buy, no-sell environment has an obvious answer (Rev. 13:17).

So if we lose the mass media outlets through which people could learn the truth during the final crisis, will the people have any protection from the overpowering delusions, aside from what a small percentage of believers can do to warn an entire world? Does God have a backup plan? As we might expect, He most assuredly does. He said in Zechariah 4:6, "'Not by might nor by power, but by My Spirit,' says the Lord of hosts" (NKJV).

Vicente Leñero, in his prologue to a Jesuit publication, says, "Drunk with power, desperate for control over its faithful, the Vatican intends to shackle us to her flock and forbid us to even think."[12] And this is an acknowledgment of what is happening even *now!* What, then, can we expect at the final crisis? In a time of religious persecution, what will religious liberty look like? Will competing religious ideas find in the mass communication media a free and open market?

"The clergy will put forth almost superhuman efforts to shut away the light lest it should shine upon their flocks. By every means at their command they will endeavor to suppress the discussion of these vital questions."[13]

We can expect a swift and determined reaction against any attempt to scatter our message.

The perfect technology for the gospel at the end-time

But what is easy to do to a TV program is not so easy to do to books. When France resorted to censoring books during the Reformation, Dutch presses stationed near the border of France ensured that book circulation continued unabated.[14]

Bob Hoskins, one of many Christian leaders who see a prominent place for Christian literature in the dissemination of the gospel, had to retreat to the written word when the government of the Islamic country in which he was preaching suddenly revoked the permit to his TV program. Hoskins explains that the public response to his program made the government nervous, and that was enough for them to ban it.[15]

Can we expect anything less during the coming global crisis? And what means can we use, in keeping with the divine counsel, to help avert the crisis?

According to Ellen White: "When the religious denominations unite with the papacy to oppress God's people, places where there is religious freedom will be opened by evangelistic canvassing."[16] And Mark Finley wonders, "Could it be that God is preparing a mighty last-day spiritual movement that will move the world, and that literature will play a significant part in God's final plans to save a last generation on Planet Earth? I am convinced that God will indeed use truth-filled literature in a mighty way during the closing work."[17]

All this indicates that literature evangelism is much more important than many in the church currently estimate. It is something far too many of us have neglected to remember and yet it will only grow in importance as circumstances narrow the path forward. As we will see in chapter 3, Scripture outlines its prophetic role.

As far back as the Protestant Reformation people regarded the book as a "divine art,"[18] and today, when we hear "increasing predictions of the end of the book as we know it,"[19] many still believe that the book "continues to be the perfect technological invention."[20] Many thinkers believe that no one will be able to kill the book, since "the book is like the spoon, the hammer, the wheel, or scissors. Once invented, nothing can improve on them."[21] To communicate information, the theory goes, books will never become obsolete as compared to other means.

Gabriel Zaid reminds us that the book's "tradition is a robust one, which has been enriched by the innovations that seemed to threaten it."[22] And from the perspective of the final crisis, when mass media outlets will be unable to freely proclaim the message, the book will live on. All this is why I suggest that the best mission strategy for the time of the end is to use the printed page, and we should be implementing it today. Mario Veloso adds, "The publishing distributed before this time will play an important role. Therefore, today we could be distributing them liberally."[23] Once the end crisis hits, it could be too late. Ellen White warns of such a danger:

"We must work while the day lasts, for when the dark night of trouble and anguish comes, it will be too late to work for God."[24]

Her statement refers to all phases of our mission.

From this brief examination we can conclude that the greatest challenge to every Adventist this side of the Second Coming is the mass distribution of the message through every means at his or her disposal. Moreover it is vital that each and every one understand that the challenge facing us is that of reaching 7 billion individuals worldwide.

It is worth noting that, according to the *Religious Freedom World Report, 2005-2005*, in 32 countries there is no religious liberty, in 48 liberty is enjoyed with difficulty, and in 128 liberty is a guarantee."[25] What does that mean to us? It means we can reach 176 countries without further ado. Now, what about the rest?

In many of the 203 countries that the Seventh-day Adventist Church has entered we have merely established our presence and have yet to reach the population. And John Graz points out that religious liberty violations are increasing and that getting the Adventist message out is getting more difficult all the time.[26] So what should we be doing right now? Will we wait until things get even more difficult? No—to do that would be to call into question the very raison d'être of our church.

I suggest that, beyond verbally preaching our message, we must spread it as never before. Furthermore we must, using all necessary precautions, distribute it even in countries that outlaw conversions. The rest is in the hands of the Holy Spirit, both now and during earth's final hours.

Intelligent decisions based only on accessible information

But how urgent should we be in getting our message out? Remember, in the final crisis hour intelligent decisions will depend entirely on the information available. Gustave Le Bon points out that "the great upheavals which precede changes of civilization . . . seem at first sight determined more especially by political transformations, foreign invasion, or the overthrow of dynasties: But more attentive study of these events shows that behind their apparent causes the real cause is generally seen to be a profound modification in the ideas of the peoples." And he adds, "The only important changes whence the renewal of civilizations results affect ideas, conceptions, and beliefs"[27] of the people. If that is so, and the idea has much research to back it up, shouldn't we be striving to get our story in front of as many as possible, given the significantly changed circumstances many now face?

If we are serious about counteracting the effect of falsehood in the final struggle, we must meet it by preempting it. Waiting until the crisis hits to proclaim the message would greatly diminish its potential redemptive impact. Alexis de Tocqueville said that "no man can struggle with advantage against the spirit of his age and country; and, however powerful he may be supposed to be, he will find it difficult to make his contemporaries share in feelings and opinions which are repugnant to all their feelings and desires."[28]

How much of the world would we be able to reach should we wait till the last possible moment before we act? Hasn't God entrusted us His message early, precisely to counteract the human tendency to procrastination? As cautioned by Ellen White: "As faithful watchmen you should see the sword coming and give the warning, that men and women may not pursue a course through ignorance that they would avoid if they knew the truth."[29]

I want to underline my belief that many of the last converts in world history will perhaps be those who were not necessarily churchgoers, who will be ignorant of basic doctrines, and who will be forced to make life-or-death choices. "The final movements will be rapid ones."[30]

It is in this context that we read Ellen White's statement that "we cannot tell what will be the results of sharing even one tract containing present truth," and "thousands in the eleventh hour will see and acknowledge the truth. . . . These conversions to truth will be made with a rapidity that will surprise the church."[31]

As a church God has made us aware that, when the time comes, our message will be proclaimed loudly and it will lead to the salvation of many:

"A good many do not see it now [the Word of God], to take their position, but these things are influencing their lives, and when the message goes with a loud voice they will be ready for it."[32]

When will this happen? According to the context it will be when the Holy Spirit will have been poured out on God's church.

Currently our publications explain many things written in the Scriptures and influence the lives of many, but they do not grasp the points well enough to make a stand for the truth. But when the message is proclaimed most fully, then, as the passage implies, infilled by the power of the Holy Spirit, they will accept the full teachings. It will bring about the situation that Ellen White described in *The Great Controversy*:

"Before the final visitation of God's judgments upon the earth there will be among the people of the Lord such a revival of primitive godliness as has not been witnessed since apostolic times. The Spirit and power of God will be poured out upon His children. At that time many will separate themselves from those churches in which the love of this world has supplanted love for God and His word. Many, both of ministers and people, will gladly accept those great truths which God has caused to be proclaimed at this time to prepare a people for the Lord's second coming. The enemy of souls desires to hinder this work; and before the time for such a movement shall come, he will endeavor to prevent it by introducing a counterfeit. . . . Under a religious guise, Satan will seek to extend his influence over the Christian world."[33]

Armageddon: the end of indecision

Our responsibility today consists in preparing the world so that it is not deceived during the war of Armageddon. And what exactly is this battle? It is "the final contest between the combined forces of Satan on one hand and Christ with His chosen and faithful followers on the other."[34]

As Jon Paulien wrote: "Armageddon is about the final proclamation of the gospel in the context of great deceptions and persecutions at the end."[35] The apostle John depicts three powerful angels who herald God's eternal gospel throughout the globe. On the other hand, we also see three unclean spirits in the form of frogs emanating from the dragon. They will attempt to disrupt the heavenly messengers' worldwide proclamation (Rev. 16:13).

"The stakes are as high as they've ever been," Paulien continued. "To the degree that God's three angels . . . reach the world, the forces of evil will have a hard time. [Conversely,] if the demonic trinity succeeds in uniting all the nations of the earth under its leadership, the final struggle of the saints will be all the more difficult."[36]

Shall we allow deception to proliferate unchecked, strengthening its earth-choking networks? And if the deception multiplies exponentially through our lack of action, will this complicate our own internal struggle in the final battle because we neglected to follow divine orders?

Armageddon itself, as we understand it, will launch "when the earth is lighted with the glory of the angel of Revelation 18, [then] the religious elements, good and evil, will awake from slumber, and the armies of the living God will take the field."[37] Ellen White also mentions the part publications will play in it:

"In a large degree through our publishing houses is to be accomplished the work of that other angel who comes down from heaven with great power, and who lightens the earth with his glory."[38]

The printed page, anointed by the Holy Spirit, is destined to play a wonderful role at earth's most decisive moment. Jon Paulien explains further:

"To be specific, three classes of people exist on earth today: . . . those who love the truth . . . those who hate the truth . . . [and] those who neither love nor hate the truth."[39] That is, the undecided.

And what is God's own attitude, given His great and loving purposes, toward those neutral ones? It is to bring indecision to an end.[40] What will you do before then, knowing that you can now have a decisive role in determining who will stand on either side of the battle?

We are told that "Armageddon . . . is a battle for the mind."[41] If so, there must be more than one opening into the fray. In fact, it means that we can intercept the enemy's efforts in a myriad of ways. A successful battle team will employ all the opportunities available to it. Today's media explosion provides countless avenues through which each one of us can individually engage in the front lines of battle. We too must use all the media weapons now at our disposal. One of the most vital, most widespread, least costly, and most readily available means is the printed page. If we are even half awake, we will notice that Satan has employed it to distract the world in a thousand different ways. We too can move steadily forward to claim many minds for truth. As a church it is our role to stand in the fray and not allow the world to be taken wholly captive, blind to the issues in the conflict. We should now distribute the third angel's message as never before so that people can have the opportunity to choose for the truth. It is both our responsibility and an unmerited privilege.

Revelation 16:13-15 shows us the devastating effects of the sixth plague. The fact that even at this late hour God continues to summon His own children shows us that when the three unclean spirits set themselves to the task of deluding a whole world, God's own preparation for Armageddon will have begun long before. It is a vital point, of which Jon Paulien wrote:

"Revelation 16:13-16 presents events that are earlier than the sixth plague, even before the close of probation."[42]

And it is here that, as a people and as a church, we can have a profound effect on an unsaved world—if we will only ratchet up the delivery of our message.

The last messenger of mercy for a world hurtling to ruin

It is certain that one of the key problems facing us in the final days will be that of seeing our evangelistic media outlets banished from the public eye. So where will the prophets be who must give a loud cry in the coming crisis? Who will play the role of the last messenger of mercy for a world hurtling to eternal ruin?

When the people of God find themselves finally forced to abandon the cities forever, it will be when the curtain begins to close on probationary time. Ellen White gives the following counsel in the context of the death decree, when it may no longer seem necessary to preach the gospel to the lost:

"As the decree issued by the various rulers of Christendom against commandment keepers shall withdraw the protection of government and abandon them to those who desire their destruction, the people of God will flee from the cities and villages and associate together in companies, dwelling in the most desolate and solitary places. Many will find refuge in the strongholds of the mountains."[43]

This faithful remnant will rapidly and completely exit the cities and villages in order to avoid the plagues about to fall on those who reject God's mercy. Others, to spare their lives, will leave beforehand.[44] God's people, divinely forewarned, will take all necessary precaution.

I wish to emphasize that as long as we remain in the cities, however, our job is to continue preaching the gospel, even under trying circumstances. Remember, "The work which the church has failed to do in a time of peace and prosperity she will have to do in a terrible crisis, under most discouraging, forbidding circumstances."[45] Therefore, why not prepare the ground beforehand, using the means currently at our disposal?

It is critical to grasp that, under the "forbidding circumstances" described above, the printed page will find easier access anywhere. Let me repeat and expand for emphasis: In the current technological environment it is relatively easy to shut down a radio, TV, or internet broadcast—but it is quite another matter to confiscate books scattered among millions of people.

Shortly before the destruction of Herod's Temple in A.D. 70 the book of Hebrews suddenly appeared. Many believe it contained just what Christians needed to stand through a fearful crisis of faith.[46] Had it not been for this epistle the primitive church might have found it much more difficult to anchor its faith in the face of such a monumental calamity. A high proportion of the believing church was still of Jewish extraction and would have surely regarded the loss of the Temple as a harbinger of impending doom for their fledgling movement. But the book of Hebrews lifted their eyes from the earthly to the heavenly temple.

In the fleeting moments just before the end many will understand for the first time the importance of Christ's Sabbath. And though "by thousands of voices, all over the earth, the warning will be given," yet "the message will be carried not so much by argument as by the deep conviction of the Spirit of God. The arguments have been presented. The seed has been sown, and now it will spring up and bear fruit. The publications distributed by missionary workers have exerted their influence."[47]

The harvest produced through the printed page during earth's last moments will be completely unexpected and therefore most impressive. The printed publication is an instrument "that can reach and influence the public mind as no other means can."[48] "It is as good and successful a method as can be employed for placing before the people the important truths for this time."[49] As Mark Finley likes to say: "For the printed page to be effective, it simply needs to be distributed."[50]

In closing, what must the church do to ensure the salvation of millions whose eternal destinies hang in the balance? Francesc X. Gelabert could not have stated it more clearly:

"The world needs urgently to know the message of the three angels.

And its printed dissemination continues to be decisive and the best base of support for all the other methods of communication."[51]

Ted N. C. Wilson, our General Conference president, says, "Now, with populations exploding in many lands and the signs of Christ's return being abundantly fulfilled throughout the earth, I envision not just a dream, but the real promise of a soaring crescendo of further evangelism and witnessing through publishing ministries at all levels and in all applications."[52]

To save the world from the fatal delusions of the end times this book not only suggests *what* we must do, but also *when, how,* and *why* it must be done. God has granted us the greatest opportunity in the world for this time. What is its prophetic significance? And who are its silent messengers?

---

[1] Ellen G. White, *Education* (Mountain View, Calif.: Pacific Press Pub. Assn., 1903), pp. 179, 180.

[2] Ellen G. White, *Testimonies for the Church* (Mountain View, Calif.: Pacific Press Pub. Assn., 1948), vol. 5, p. 463. (Italics supplied.)

[3] Ellen G. White, *The Great Controversy* (Mountain View, Calif.: Pacific Press Pub. Assn., 1911), p. 590.

[4] *Ibid.,* p. 615.

[5] *Ibid.,* p. 612.

[6] Ellen G. White, *Selected Messages* (Washington, D.C.: Review and Herald Pub. Assn., 1958, 1980), book 1, p. 118. (Italics supplied.)

[7] *Adult Sabbath School Bible Study Guide,* April-June, 2012, pp. 2, 3.

[8] www.articleswave.com/articles/reasons-for-media-censorship.html.

[9] E. G. White, *The Great Controversy,* p. 592.

[10] Ellen G. White, *Last Day Events* (Nampa, Idaho: Pacific Press Pub. Assn., 1992), p. 12.

[11] Herbert N. Foerstel, *Banned in the Media* (Westport, Conn.: Greenwood Press, 1998), pp. ix, x.

[12] In Enrique Maza, *La Libertad de Expresión en la Iglesia* [*Freedom of Expression in the Church*] (México D.F.: Editorial Océano de México, S. A. de C. V., 2006), p. 11.

[13] E. G. White, *The Great Controversy,* p. 607.

[14] Lucien Febvre and Henry-Jean Martin, *La Aparición del Libro* [*The Coming of the Book*] (México D.F.: Fondo de Cultura Económica, 2005), p. 287.

[15] Bob and Rob Hoskins, *Affect Destiny* (Pompano, Fla.: Book of Hope, 2003), p. 6.

[16] E. G. White, *Colporteur Ministry,* p. 11.

[17] Mark Finley, "When Hope Comes Alive," *The Literature Evangelist,* January-March 2010, p. 3, http://publishing.gc.adventist.org/files/pdf/LEMIssue690.pdf.

[18] Febvre and Martin, p. 383.

[19] Andrew Taylor, *Books That Changed the World* (China: Quercus, 2008), p. 5.

[20] Manuel Pimentel, *Manual del Editor* [Editor's Manual] (Córdova, España: Berenice, 2007), p. 67.

[21] Umberto Eco and Jean-Claude Carriere, *Nadia Acabara con los Libros* [*No One Will Kill the Book*] (Barcelona, España: Random House Mondadori, 2010), p. 10.

[22] Gabriel Zaid, *So Many Books: Reading and Publishing in the Age of Abundance,* trans. Natasha Wimmer (Philadelphia: Paul Dry Books, 2005), p. 10.

[23] Mario Veloso, *Apocalipsis y el Fin Del Mundo* [*Revelation and the End of the World*]

(Nampa, Idaho: Pacific Press Pub. Assn., 1998), p. 224. Examines the context of the word "before" in Mark 13:10. Reina Valera Antigua.

[24] Ellen G. White, *Early Writings* (Washington, D.C.: Review and Herald Pub. Assn., 1882), p. 48.

[25] See John Graz, http://news.adventist.org/en/archive/articles/2005/07/18/world-church-religious-freedom-status-documented-in-report/.

[26] *Ibid.*

[27] Gustave Le Bon, *The Crowd* (Mineola, N.Y.: Dover Publications, 2002), p. ix.

[28] Alexis de Tocqueville, *Democracy in America,* trans. Henry Reeve (Cambridge, Mass.: Sever and Francis, 1863), vol. 2, p. 313. Example: When King Saul thought to kill Jonathan, the people would not hear of it (1 Sam. 14:45).

[29] E. G. White, *Last Day Events,* p. 127.

[30] E. G. White, *Testimonies,* vol. 9, p. 11.

[31] E. G. White, *Last Day Events,* p. 212.

[32] *Ibid.*

[33] E. G. White, *The Great Controversy,* p. 464.

[34] Hans K. LaRondelle, "Armageddon: Sixth and Seventh Plagues," *Symposium on Revelation,* ed. Frank B. Holbrook (Silver Spring, Md.: Biblical Research Institute, 1992), book 2, p. 377.

[35] Jon Paulien, *Armageddon at the Door* (Hagerstown, Md.: Autumn House Publishing, 2008), p. 120.

[36] *Ibid.*, p. 140.

[37] Ellen G. White manuscript 175, 1899, in Ellen G. White, *Manuscript Releases* (Silver Spring, Md.: Ellen G. White Estate, 1993), vol. 19, p. 160.

[38] E. G. White, *Christian Service,* p. 148.

[39] Paulien, p. 79.

[40] *Ibid.*

[41] *Ibid.*, p. 120. (Italics supplied.)

[42] *Ibid.*, p. 141.

[43] E. G. White, *The Great Controversy,* p. 626.

[44] We are told that before the end of probationary time "the two armies will stand distinct and separate, and this distinction will be so marked that many who shall be convinced of truth will come on the side of God's commandment-keeping people. When this grand work is to take place in the battle, prior to the last closing conflict, many will be imprisoned, many will flee for their lives from cities and towns, and many will be martyrs for Christ's sake in standing in defense of the truth" (E. G. White, *Maranatha,* p. 199). God can surely be counted on to guide us individually, directing according to each individual's circumstances.

[45] E. G. White, *Christian Service,* p. 158.

[46] See *The Seventh-day Adventist Bible Commentary* (Washington, D.C.: Review and Herald Pub. Assn., 1957), vol. 7, pp. 388, 389.

[47] E. G. White, *The Great Controversy,* p. 612.

[48] E. G. White, *Colporteur Ministry,* p. 149.

[49] *Ibid.*, p. 7.

[50] Finley, "When Hope Comes Alive."

[51] Francesc X. Gelabert, "Art and Science of Writing," translated from *Ministerio Adventista,* November-December 2009, p. 27.

[52] Ted N. C. Wilson, "A Personal Letter From Our World Church President," *The Literature Evangelist,* January-March 2011.

Chapter 2

Silent Prophets in the Eye of the Storm

Y2K came, and nothing happened. Those who believed that the end of the world would occur at the millennium's end were terribly disappointed. No catastrophes or cataclysms arose. Computers kept on humming, and the predicted global chaos amounted to nothing more than speculation.[1] More than a decade has passed, and everything seems to indicate that we will have to wait even further. Five, 10, or 20 more years—who knows? What is Jesus waiting for? Is there some prophetic significance to the "tense calm" we enjoy today, despite the difficult economic conditions? There is. And what you are about to discover is that Jesus is coming soon—*much sooner than you dare imagine.*

You may have heard of "hurricane hunters." They are reconnaissance planes of the U.S. Air Force specially designed for the hurricane season. The spouses of such pilots classify what their husband or wives do as "harebrained" and confess that every time they leave for duty, they wonder if it will be the last goodbye, *because these pilots fly a plane across the hurricane.* The instruments they carry record such things as wind velocity, atmospheric pressure, temperature, humidity, and direction of movement. And though they are flying specially equipped planes, the pilots still risk their lives every time they go up.

Once the planes reach the hurricanes, they must circle in place. But they have nothing to worry about there. The eye of a hurricane has a deceptive calm—it contains no fog, rain, or wind.[2] The pilot then releases a type of weather balloon that, as it falls, transmits signals to the National Hurricane Center in Miami, Florida. In most cases the data gleaned enables weather forecasters to help prevent further destruction.[3]

Being in the eye of the storm, then, is vital to knowing which direction it is traveling. Radio signals sent from that position can mean the difference between life and death when the storm strikes land. But not any plane can accomplish the mission. A commercial airliner could never make it. Yet it is a most important work. Amelia Ebhardt, a hurricane hunter copilot, says, "We help people to be prepared for the storms, which in turn saves lives."[4]

Surrounded in the eye of the storm of Revelation 7

What's the spiritual link, you ask? The Bible predicts something very similar will happen in our time. The apostle John sees an angel having the seal of the living God, who orders the four angels stationed at the four winds to "*hurt not the earth, neither the sea, nor the trees*, till we have sealed the servants of our God in their foreheads" (Rev. 7:3).

The language employed here echoes that of hurricane reconnaissance. God commissions His angels to make (prior to the end of probation and Christ's return) an eye of the hurricane large enough to contain the earth. The expression "that the wind should not blow" (verse 1) indicates that it is a time of relative calm. And from within this calm the Lord is transmitting the final signal of all: something we could categorize as "peace and safety," but followed by sudden destruction:

"Angels are now restraining the winds of strife, that they may not blow until the world shall be warned of its coming doom; *but a storm is gathering*, ready to burst upon the earth; and when God shall bid His angels loose the winds, there will be such a scene of strife as no pen can picture."[5] We are in the eye of the hurricane.

Jacques B. Doukhan noted that the *chiastic* structure (ABA') of the aforementioned passage "identifies *the survivors*" of the current crisis. He sees three movements in John's description of what happens *during* the sealing. "The first action (A) spares the earth, sea, and trees (Rev. 7:1). The second action (B) threatens the earth and the sea (verse 2). And the third action (A') again spares the earth, sea, and trees (verse 3)." And his conclusion: "The center of the *chiasm* reveals the element of nature spared by the winds," and that is, "the trees are the sole survivors of the disaster."[6]

Since the trees represent the righteous (Ps. 1:3), it shows that they, together with the wicked, still run the risk of complacency because they are in the center—in the eye—of the cosmic hurricane, where there is no fog, no wind, and no blinding rains. *The winds are stayed*, but the danger looms large because "the other half" of the hurricane threatens a people who believe that they have already weathered the worst of the storm.

The tenth chapter of Revelation suggests the same sequence. There we see an angel with a book in his hand, and when he speaks (which happens between the sixth and seventh trumpet, parallel to the sealing that takes place between the sixth and seventh seals), seven thunders (of whose recording is forbidden) utter their voices with a message of judgment. What does it mean? Hans K. LaRondelle explains that "the command to 'seal up' the content of the seven thunders may indicate that *no longer will there come warning judgments,* in view of the foreknowledge that *such judgments do not lead the people to repentance. . . .* The final judgments come *only after* probationary time has ended, as the seven last plagues."[7]

In other words, before the end of probation, no matter what happens, people will persist in the idea that nothing remarkable is taking place. What's the use of recording the message of the seven thunders? It is not necessary. No matter the events, they seem *irrelevant* to most. This is what we are currently witnessing. And that in itself constitutes our warning as to the time we are now living in. It is vitally important, then, that we be about the business of preparing the people. We must warn them against complacency. Probation will end for a world fast asleep.

The literary form of the book of Revelation suggests that prior to the final judgments we will have to be in the eye of the hurricane.[8] Scripture presents our current moment as being in the center, inside a giant parenthesis *surrounded by warnings of the impending judgments, followed by the final judgment itself.* The sequence includes seven churches, seven seals, and seven trumpets, and each of them *ends* with the second coming of Christ. "These apocalyptic endings of each chain indicate that the three series are not three chronological sequences, each following the other. Rather they repeat the same historical sequence. . . . *This creates an increasing urgency* in the Apocalypse."

Then, quoting Robert H. Mounce, LaRondelle wrote:

"Each new vision *intensifies the realization of coming judgment. Like a mounting storm at sea* each new crest of the wave moves history closer to its final destiny."[9]

And we are situated in the eye of the storm—an oasis of calm.

Stephen N. Haskell indicated that when Europe was in the middle of seemingly endless political and social strife, and especially during the French Revolution, almost overnight, "in the midst of the turmoil and strife, *came a sudden calm.* No man could assign any reason for it. Like the troubled waters of Gennesaret when Christ spoke peace out of the storm, *tumult and confusion ceased.* The four angels had been stationed on the earth to stay the winds of strife till the servants of God could be sealed."[10]

Now, what is "the other half" of the coming storm if we are currently in the eye of the hurricane? As we have already seen, Ellen White has explained that a storm is indeed gathering. Can we know for certain what it is and how near it may be? To find out, we must first determine the shape of the tempest already past to recognize the one just ahead.

The medieval church generally directed the "first part" of the storm. The development of Christendom, with all its conflicts through the year 1798, was principally its own doing. As such, we can expect the coming strife to likewise involve the participation of this power.

In an official Adventist document we read the following:

"Adventists believe, on the basis of biblical predictions, that just prior to the second coming of Christ this earth will experience a period of unprecedented turmoil, with the seventh-day Sabbath as a focal point. In that context, we expect that world religions—including the major Christian bodies as key players—will align themselves with the forces in opposition to God and to the Sabbath."[11] Which world religions might that include?

Tim Roosenberg, in his excellent book *Islam and Christianity in Prophecy,* defines Daniel 11's king of the north, the last great archenemy in the final sorties of the powers of evil, as "geopolitical powers" of "Western Christianity," headed up by "the Papacy,"[12] which is in harmony with Ellen White's statements that the people of God will have to confront "agencies combined against the truth."[13] And this same power manifests itself as "a whirlwind" (Dan. 11:40) against the truth of God and His Sabbath.

The dire implication for us as a church is that those not standing for the sealing while still in the eye of the hurricane will, when the mark of the beast materializes, risk receiving the mark and the seven last plagues. And the world? It faces the danger of believing that all is business as usual.

The deaf ears of the world

A traveler would occasionally visit his friend who made a living as a blacksmith. Once he noticed how the man's dog, who lay nearby, would let out a bark with every blow on the anvil. But when he returned some years later, he noticed an interesting change: The animal no longer barked when the hammer struck the anvil. He asked his friend why the dog no longer responded to the strike of the hammer. The blacksmith explained that because it was always at his side and exposed to constant noise, the dog had become deaf. In a way, the dog was still in the eye of the storm— but even if the metalwork around him were being blown to bits, it would seem as nothing to the animal.

The Bible warns us about the mind-set of the last days in our world's history. Though disaster appears in different places, the apostle Peter says, "Knowing this first, that there shall come in the last days scoffers . . . saying, Where is the promise of his coming? for since the fathers fell asleep, *all things continue as they were from the beginning of the creation*" (2 Peter 3:3, 4). The fact that the world is being rent to pieces will have no special significance to the people living on earth. Their attitude will be "business as usual."

Jon Paulien explains that "both Jesus and Paul portray the last days as somewhat *normal* times, in spite of all the spectacular events." And even though a crisis will appear before the final end, Paulien makes it clear that "the normalcy will seem that way *only to those without the eyes of Christian faith.*"[14]

The moment you never expected now returns

Jesus warned about such a mind-set when He said, "But as the days of [Noah] were, *so shall also* the coming of the Son of man be." But what were the days of Noah really like? "For as in the days that were *before* the flood they were eating and drinking, marrying and giving in marriage, until the day that [Noah] entered into the ark, *and knew not until the flood came, and took them all away*; so shall also the coming of the Son of man be" (Matt. 24:37-39).

The antediluvians (those alive before the Flood) perished because, among other reasons, they thought it was all "business as usual." In a certain sense, they were right—before then things had continued on as they always had. And *precisely such an environment existed* when the final destruction struck. So Jesus warned us that there will be a repeat of this same experience. Humanity will once more become complacent. The Son of man will come *at "an hour as ye think not"* (verse 44).

Imagine the scene: It is business as usual when God tells Noah that it is time to board the ark. The period of waiting has ended. The opportunity has gone forever. Now Noah walks into the ark. The first day comes and goes, and nothing unusual happens. The second day, again nothing happens. Third day, no change. Fourth, fifth, sixth days . . . nothing. Seventh day: sudden and unexpected destruction (Gen. 7:10). The most amazing thing to recognize is that even after Noah was well inside the ark, *even then* nothing unusual took place—at least not for an uncomfortable seven days. God announced the end of probationary time and Noah entered the ark, but even then things remained the same—at least for a short time. The antediluvians were in the eye of the storm, but they never knew the difference. Now note: Jesus warned that events will repeat themselves. But where was it already prophesied?

God will hold back partial punishment for only so long

The prophet Zephaniah, called to proclaim the end of the whole world (Zeph. 1:2), spoke of the mental condition at the time of the end, saying, "And it shall come to pass at that time, that I will . . . punish the men that are settled on their lees: that say in their heart, The Lord will not do good, neither will he do evil" (verse 12). Referring to how close the day of the Lord is, "and hasteth greatly" (verse 14), the prophet warns that before it arrives people will reassure themselves that nothing out of the ordinary is taking place. Yet very suddenly God "shall make even a speedy riddance of all them that dwell in the land" (verse 18).

We see then, that the beginning of the idea of an irrevocable decision to make a "speedy riddance" *of all the living* is within the context of apparent calm. The Lord says, "I have cut off the nations: their towers are desolate; I made their streets waste. . . . I said, Surely thou wilt fear me, thou wilt receive instruction, . . . but they rose early, and corrupted all their doings. Therefore wait ye upon me, saith the Lord, *until the day that I rise up to the prey*: for my determination is to gather the nations, that I may assemble the kingdoms, to pour upon them mine indignation, even all my fierce anger: for *all the earth* shall be devoured with the fire of my jealousy" (Zeph. 3:6-8).

Notice that it all happens in the context of judgment, very similar to what Revelation states about the great harlot who, prophetically speaking, receives all her plagues *in one day*. In fact, John emphasized the speed of judgment by saying that *in one hour* the harlot will be judged, made desolate, and burned (Rev. 18:8, 10, 17, 19).

Did you notice that even when the world goes right on sinning, the Lord will not mete out immediate punishment? I suggest that He is asking us to look for His coming in what, to the lost, will be a seemingly deceptive environment—when the wicked will think everything is business as usual. Paradoxically, it will lead them on to greater evil:

"Because sentence against an evil work is not executed speedily, therefore the heart of the sons of men is fully set in them to do evil" (Eccl. 8:11).

Evil will go on from bad to worse, as we are witnessing now. Painful as it will be, before the end of probation we will witness strange behavior that will not receive immediate punishment. For that reason we will be forced to await the coming of the Lord even as His judgments are delayed. Notice: His coming is not delayed, but His judgments. In other words, before the destruction we must pass through the eye of the hurricane. It is as if God's great mercy was, in effect, preparing the wicked for the final punishment. It sounds strange, but that is truly as it is. God will destroy the world not in sections but by one single blow. In the meantime, everyone will imagine that things will go on as usual. Here is a recurring theme in Scripture.

Before the final destruction, unprecedented prosperity

Recall the parable of the wheat and the tares. Jesus said the *harvest* is the end of the world (Matt. 13:39). Now, what happens *just before* the destruction of the tares? Is God aware of just how evil (the tares) is proliferating? Yes, He knows fully, and He *deliberately allows it to grow unchecked.* God intends that the tares mature together with the wheat. To the servant's question "Wilt thou then that we go and gather them up?" the Lord answers, "Nay. . . . *Let both grow* together *until the harvest*" (verses 28-30).

Even though the winds have been checked so that they do not hurt the earth or the sea, the end is at the door. The ripening harvest of evil will be the biggest proof of the soon return of Jesus, as illustrated by Paul's statement:

"But evil men and seducers shall wax worse and worse, deceiving, and being deceived" (2 Tim. 3:13).

They believe that no matter what vices they indulge, no retribution will come. And yet the reason the Lord allows the ripening evil to grow unchecked is that He wishes that no one "should perish, but that all should come to repentance" (2 Peter 3:9).

We see the ripening of evil just prior to the final destruction prefigured in the Exodus of the children of Israel en route to the Promised Land. God told Abraham that his people would be enslaved in a strange land and would not proceed to the Promised Land until the wickedness of the Amorites should reach its zenith (Gen. 15:16). Of course, this delay would not change the ultimate outcome, but it would ensure that the wicked would indeed continue on in evil until God had to destroy them. To the Amorites, however, everything was business as usual.

Ellen White, commenting on the parable of the importunate widow and the unrighteous judge, noted that "from age to age the Lord has made known the manner of His working," and that "*When a crisis has come, He has revealed Himself.* . . . With nations, with families, and with individuals, He has often permitted matters to come to a crisis, that His interference might become marked. . . . *In this time of prevailing iniquity* we may know that the last great crisis is at hand."[15]

It is worth nothing that Jesus applied the parable to the time of the end and said, "And shall not God avenge his own elect . . . though he bear long with them? . . . He will avenge them speedily. Nevertheless when the Son of man cometh, shall he find faith on the earth?" (Luke 18:7, 8). That is, until the great final crisis explodes on the scene, the world and even the church will come to think that all is business as usual. Note that Luke presented the parable in the context of end-time events (Luke 17:20-37). Are we fully conscious of the time in which we live? Indeed, we are in the eye of the hurricane!

Ironically, Jesus also said, "Ye can discern the face of the sky; but can ye not discern the signs of the times?" (Matt. 16:3). And He qualified as hypocrites those who, during His first advent, were positioned so as to know the times, yet demanded a sign in spite of the overabundance of evidence surrounding them (Luke 11:16, 29).

I propose that God will also call to account the final generation just before Jesus returns. The world *will believe that everything is business as usual* in spite of the evidence of signs and wonders. They refuse to believe Jesus' coming is at the door.

We note the same principle in the parable of the fig tree. Before its destruction the fig tree *received good treatment it should not have had were it not for unmerited grace*. It had been amply proven not to give fruit (and it never produced any), yet to the end it had the benefit of a vinedresser keeping and caring for it (Luke 13:8). It received as much a chance as possible to bear fruit.

And how many there are today who think they are in good standing before God because they receive His blessings, even though they produce no fruit! It is a fatal deception. In the case of the fig tree, *it was business as usual*—except that was to be the final attention it would receive. Grace was making its final call. *Blessings increased prior to the final destruction.*

The "reappearance" of Samson in the end-time

The Jews of Jesus' time suffered the same experience as had Samson centuries before. You will remember that it was forbidden for him to marry a woman who was not an Israelite, yet he did. In spite of that, his *strength did not ebb* (Judges 14:6). What must he have thought? *I can break God's law, and things will go on as usual.* Much of the world will assume the same thing just before Jesus returns.

As a Jew and a Nazarite, Samson was also not to touch the bodies of dead animals. Yet he chose to eat the honey from a honeycomb that lay inside the carcass of a lion he had previously killed. Again, his strength did not leave him (verse 19; Judges 15:16). Once more he reasoned, *I can do whatever I please, and it will be business as usual.* But he was in the eye of the hurricane.

Ellen White tells us that "it is the restraining power of God that prevents mankind from passing fully under the control of Satan." And further, "God does not stand toward the sinner as an executioner of the sentence against transgression; but He leaves the rejectors of His mercy to themselves, to reap that which they have sown."[16] In the meantime, all is well—business as usual.

Samson also knew that he should not consort with prostitutes, but he decided that was not to be a hindrance. He "went . . . to Gaza, and saw there an harlot, and went in unto her" (Judges 16:1). Would he now be abandoned and left to his destruction? No. Surrounded by Philistines, he "arose at midnight, and took the doors of the gate of the city, and the two posts, and went away with them, bar and all, and put them upon his shoulders, and carried them up to the top of an hill that is before Hebron" (verse 3). What must Samson have thought then? From that hill he could see all of Hebron, the *land of giants* (Joshua 15:8, 13). It must have seemed to him that he was the greatest of them.

Imagine the scene: Samson is up at midnight, reasoning to himself, *I am getting better and better. Look at where I am!* Business as usual. But his end was creeping nearer and nearer. When he finally fell into Delilah's hands, he said, "I will go out as at other times before, and shake myself. And *he wist not that the Lord was departed from him*" (Judges 16:20).

Can you see what self-deception we can fall into when we assume that all is business as usual? Destruction will strike when we least expect it. As Solomon said: "Though a sinner do evil an hundred times, and his days be prolonged, yet surely I know that . . . *it shall not be well with the wicked*" (Eccl. 8:12, 13). They may congratulate self, but annihilation looms over them.

Remember the inhabitants of Jericho in Joshua's time. Judgment had come for the Canaanites, but ensconced within their walls, they felt secure. Israel went the first time around the walls, and nothing happened. Business as usual. Second day, nothing. Third day. Nothing. Fourth, fifth, sixth days

. . . still nothing. Unbeknown to them, *they were in the eye of the hurricane.* Seventh day? First circuit, nothing. Second . . . still nothing. Then third, fourth, fifth, sixth . . . nothing had changed. But on the seventh time . . .

Such a business-as-usual mind-set that persists even in the face of looming destruction presents itself every time judgment arrives, no matter the era. Today we *are* living at the time of the end. Why would it be any different?

Who pays the false prophets?

But something definitely contributes to the idea of "business as usual," spreading the notion that there is nothing to be afraid of. It is in the interest of most politicians to make people believe that their administration is *good* government. To do otherwise would mean the loss of power. Therefore, no matter how poor their management, they have an army of public relations experts charged with selling us the idea that all is well, that nothing bad will happen—all to hang on to power. What political faction wants to yield its place to its competition? No earthly government will ever say, "Be concerned; we are not governing well."

Prior to the destruction of Jerusalem in A.D. 70, the counterparts of today's politicians, "to establish their power more firmly, . . . *bribed false prophets* to proclaim . . . that the people were to wait for deliverance from God. To the last, multitudes held fast to the belief that the Most High would interpose for the defeat of their adversaries. But Israel had spurned the divine protection, *and now she had no defense.*"[17]

False prophets foster the illusion that all is well. Who doesn't want to hear that things will get better and that abundance is right around the corner? Wouldn't we rather live in a world in which prosperity reigns? Of course. And such will be the mental condition of the world just prior to the end.

In response to the business-as-usual idea that all is actually well, Christ, foreseeing our day, said, "*Then* shall the kingdom of heaven be likened unto ten virgins, which took their lamps, and went forth to meet the bridegroom. And five of them were wise, and five were foolish" (Matt. 25:1, 2). Now, what was the foolish ones' problem, *since they too knew that the bridegroom was coming*? It is an issue of *complacency.* "Business as usual" is only an illusion. We are now in the eye of the hurricane. As a result, what should our work be?

The times in which we live tell us plainly—we must proclaim that

Jesus is coming soon. Now, what can we do to be in tune with a period in which everything is seemingly "business as usual"? Is there a work the church can undertake in such a context, one that we could label as "Silent Prophets in the Eye of the Storm"? Among the current chief labors of the church is that of publishing. Such a ministry has always been "in the eye of the hurricane" and is the only one that has been silently reminding Satan that his time is short (Rev. 12:12). Good, but does the concept have a biblical foundation?

A silent, Bible-based message

In fact, Scripture contains references to a silent testimony. In the Gospel of Mark we find a leprous man whom Jesus heals, then commands to witness silently for the benefit of a special class. The Word says that Jesus "straitly charged him" to say nothing to anyone, but to show himself to the priest and offer his purification gift according to Moses' injunction. All this would be "for a testimony unto them" (Mark 1:43-45).

Here we see Jesus inviting the man to present a silent witness, but one based on the written Word—what "Moses commanded." It was a silent witness with the purpose of showing the priests that Jesus was the Messiah.

This instance fittingly illustrates the ministry of the printed page. First, because it constitutes a silent messenger, and second, because our books and periodicals reflect Scripture. It is exactly what Jesus asked the newly healed man to do.

Jesus could have instructed him to proclaim loudly what He had done for him. After all, wouldn't it be only natural that a healed man would want to tell everyone about his benefactor? But Jesus asked him to remain silent and gave him a specific witnessing assignment.

Jesus also used this method when He sent the formerly demon-possessed Gadarene to "tell his own" what great things God had done for him (Mark 5:19). But this time it was different. The Lord who knows how to plan had a different approach. Jesus wanted the leper's witness to be a silent testimony. But, disregarding a direct order from He who makes the very best plans, the man went and told all (Mark 1:45).

Some will sympathize with the leper by arguing that, given the greatness of the miracle, he really had no other option but to shout it from the housetops. But the fact remains that Jesus told him otherwise—the Savior desired a silent testimony based directly on Scripture.

It may not seem like a big deal to go against Jesus' commands in this way. However, we should ever keep in mind that in so doing, we might actually be aiding the destroyer instead of assisting Christ. Mark's account of the story ends this way: "Jesus could no more openly enter into the city, but was without in desert places."

Though it is difficult at times to comply with Christ's commands, to decide not to do it is really a matter of unbelief. We refuse to accept His plans when not synonymous with our own, or we refuse to believe that His is truly a better, more prudent way to proceed. Instead, we want to work out our method first. And often we do not reason that maybe God's plan involves more than one method, all of them included in His perfectly designed approach.

A little-known lesson from the Japanese bamboo plant

An insight drawn from God's book of nature may help us to understand better the power of the printed page in the end-times. Before Japanese farmers can plant bamboo, they must first prepare the soil by fertilizing and irrigating, making certain the ground is ready. After ridding the area of pests and rocks, they next weed, fertilize, and irrigate some more. Then they can place the plant in the seedbed. However, after many weeks little evidence is seen that the plants have any intention of germinating. Corn normally sprouts after eight days, but with bamboo, entire *months* go by without any signs of life. The first six months pass without any shoots. Even after nine months you don't notice any change—*no apparent growth.* And yet the farmers must keep working day after day, week after week. They would make a big mistake if they slacked off once the process was under way. In truth, they must demonstrate great patience to see the results of their labor.

A whole year goes by, but nothing emerges from the soil. It is as if the bare ground were completely ignoring the farmers' efforts. But they persistently trudge on.

An onlooker might conclude that nothing requires more faith than becoming a bamboo farmer. And can we blame them? It is an extraordinary plant. One could say its cultivation seems designed to awaken doubt, resentment, and skepticism (as happens in the area of publishing). But Japanese farmers are an intelligent lot, and they are not overcome by feelings or fleeting impressions. A second year goes by and then a third, yet still nothing breaks the surface of the ground. An amateur farmer might conclude that wisdom would demand planting another crop to stop wasting time and effort. But bamboo farmers keep the big picture in mind. They cannot effectively produce otherwise.

Four years go by, and not one of the bamboo farmers have let go of the hope of harvest. Though the earth remains bare, none of them lose patience or curse the ground. Time continues its march, and the fifth and sixth years pass. So what is happening? After much fertilizing, water, and care, the plant shows not a whit of hope. Some might think the seeds were sterile, or the ground poor, or both. But then *in the seventh year* there appears in the seedbed a shoot of what will become an extraordinary plant. Once that happens, things really take off!

In surprising fashion bamboo, like asparagus, develops in a way that one can almost see it grow by the hour. Some plants reach 100 feet in height in only 12 to 15 weeks. The long wait and diligent effort receive more than ample reward.

The power of root growth

So what, if anything, has happened in those six long gestation years when nothing showed above ground? The bamboo plant has been spreading invisibly and rapidly beneath the earth's surface. It was silently producing a powerful root system that later helped it grow to amazing heights in a short time. It is true that in order to build high, one must start with a good foundation. That describes precisely the development of the bamboo plant. So what's the moral of this story?

Just this: When typhoons beat mercilessly on Japanese coasts and drag everything away, especially tree roots and plants of all kinds, one plant remains unmovable. It may bend beneath hurricane winds, but it quickly returns to its elegant vertical position once the storm has exhausted its fury. That is the story of Japanese bamboo. No matter how hard the wind may blow, it simply will not uproot bamboo. It grows out of sight before any visible development so that no storm can lay it waste.[18]

This lesson from the Japanese bamboo growth process dovetails with what our instructors in publishing have been trying for so long to teach: The printed page will play a key role in the final crisis, and will be one of the last standing ministries.

The corollary is that *we cannot expect the books, tracts, and magabooks we distribute to bear fruit immediately or constantly from one day to the next.* Think of books as time bombs, which do not explode at impact but at a predetermined time set by divine intelligence.

Today the printed page is growing an impressive root system, and every single one of us should be supremely interested in seeing that these roots are sufficiently robust to withstand the struggles of the coming crisis. Our work is simply to disseminate our message abundantly.

You and I, like the hurricane hunter planes, are now situated in the eye of the storm and should be signaling the world with the message of Christ's soon return. The explosive spreading of the gospel is the single greatest sign of His soon coming (Matt. 24:14). Everything about us may look to be business as usual, yet Christ is at the door. But *how* will the ripening happen?

As Ellen White explained: "These silent messengers are enlightening and molding the minds of thousands in every country and in every clime."[19] And she adds: "More than one thousand will soon be converted in one day, *most of whom will trace their first convictions to the reading of our publications.*"[20]

The question begs to be asked: Who will have distributed all those saving pages? Whose hands will achieve such wide-reaching results? Is it up to me and you? That is the Lord's hope.

Do the spreading of these silent messengers really fulfill a specific prophecy? And if so, which one? Keep reading and find out.

---

[1] "El Y2K no Generó el Caos, sólo Polémica" ["Y2K Generated No Chaos, Only Polemics"], www.lanacion.com.ar/nota.asp?nota_id=37724.

[2] Steve Chapple, "Into the Eye of a Hurricane," *Reader's Digest*, November 2009, pp. 115, 116.

[3] "A Visit to the Hurricane-chasing Plane 2009," http://smn.cna.gob.mx/eventos/cazahuracanes09.pdf.

[4] In Chapple, p. 117.

[5] E. G. White, *Education*, pp. 179, 180. (Italics supplied.)

[6] Jacques B. Doukhan, *Secrets of Revelation: The Apocalypse Through Hebrew Eyes* (Hagerstown, Md.: Review and Herald Pub. Assn., 2002), p. 69. (Italics supplied.)

[7] Hans K. LaRondelle, *How to Understand the End-Time Prophecies of the Bible* (Sarasota, Fla.: First Impressions, 1997), p. 197. (Italics supplied.)

[8] Revelation has the structure of a seven-branched candlestick. The sealing is in the center.

[9] LaRondelle, p. 103. (Italics supplied.)

[10] Stephen N. Haskell, *The Story of the Seer of Patmos* (Nashville: Southern Pub. Assn., 1905), p. 132. (Italics supplied.)

[11] http://adventist.org/beliefs/statements/main-stat42.html.

[12] See Tim Roosenberg and Tim Lale, *Islam and Christianity in Prophecy* (Hagerstown, Md.: Review and Herald Pub. Assn., 2011), pp. 9, 12, 37, 45. On the other hand, Jacques B. Doukhan points out that "the story of the north-south conflict in Daniel 11:5-45 is the

same as that of the little horn of chapter 8" (*Secrets of Daniel* [Hagerstown, Md.: Review and Herald Pub. Assn., 2000], pp. 169, 170). This means that one of the powers manifesting itself as a whirlwind in the time of the end is none other than the Papacy, otherwise known, in Daniel 11, as the king of the north.

[13] E. G. White, *The Great Controversy,* p. 612.

[14] Jon Paulien, "Indicators of the End Time: Are the 'Signs' Really Signs?" *Ministry,* June-July 2000. (Italics supplied.)

[15] Ellen G. White, *Christ's Object Lessons* (Washington, D.C.: Review and Herald Pub. Assn., 1900), p. 178. (Italics supplied.)

[16] E. G. White, *The Great Controversy,* p. 36.

[17] *Ibid.*, p. 29.

[18] Adapted from Pedro Morales Satizábal, *Aprendiendo a Vivir* [*Learning How to Live*] (México D.F.: Gema Editores/Agencia de Publicaciones México Central A.C., 2007), pp. 79, 80.

[19] E. G. White, *Colporteur Ministry,* p. 5.

[20] *Ibid.*, p. 151. (Italics supplied.)

Chapter 3

Prophets of the Final Sealing

Literature will be among the last standing ministries the Lord will use to finish His redemptive work on earth. But is the printed page, in its simple approach, powerful enough to help finish the work of sealing those who will be saved? Do you know *what* the sealing is and how it will actually happen? Have you pondered the idea that some book you may have sold or given away *could one day be the final preacher to someone on earth* and that you are participating in the most important prophecy of our time? Consider this:

"When the religious denominations unite with the papacy to oppress God's people, places *where there is religious freedom will be opened by evangelistic canvassing.*"[1]

Could this quote be the sole source of support that publishing will be among the ministries to finish the spreading of the gospel before Jesus comes? It is not. As a student literature evangelist I would frequently hear that we would be among the last to leave the scene of battle. I searched hard for the biblical and Ellen G. White support behind that thought, but at the time the only thing I could come up with was the above quote. But there is so much more! I would like to illustrate what is going to happen through an event that took place just a few years ago.

An event prophesied more than 100 years before

In 1999 the heading of a bulletin sitting on a counter at the North Mexican Mission office startled me. It said, "Saint Thomas Becomes Seventh-day Adventist." I took the bait and leaned over for a closer look. In my mind I thought, *Isn't Saint Thomas a Catholic?* And then: *Isn't he the most distinguished theologian in the Catholic Church who lived during the thirteenth century? What is Saint Thomas doing on the premises of the Adventist Church, and converted, to boot?*

Since at that time I was head of the publishing department for the

North Mexican Mission in Chihuahua, Mexico, I naturally wanted to learn all about the intriguing incident, especially since it involved one of our books. It turned out that some years ago one of our literature evangelists had placed books at an evangelical church in a region of the state of Chihuahua called Santo Tomas. The church's leadership had read them. Though impressed with what they found in them, they made no changes in what they were doing.

However, 15 years later Pope John Paul II's encyclical *Dies Domini,* in which he calls the world back to observance of Sunday,[2] had startled them. The evangelical church's leaders recognized that this event fulfilled sections of *The Great Controversy* that they had read years before. In response they sought out a member of the Seventh-day Adventist Church to learn more. The Adventist church member called on his pastor, who in turn contacted the evangelist for the North Mexican Mission, who, after completing a one-week prophecy series at the church, baptized the first group of its members. Another group baptism soon followed. Today it is a Seventh-day Adventist congregation.

In the not-too-distant future Adventist publishing will play a similar role, but on a far vaster scale. Referring to *The Great Controversy,* Ellen White states:

"The results of the circulation of this book are not to be judged by what now appears. By reading it, some souls will be aroused, and will have courage to unite themselves at once with those who keep the commandments of God. But a much larger number who read it *will not take their position until they see the very events taking place that are foretold in it.*"[3]

That is precisely what played out in the town of Santo Tomas.

We might be forgiven for thinking that today nothing of any consequence is happening as a result of publishing—that all is "business as usual." But such thinking is clearly mistaken. The silent prophets carry on their work in the same way as Japanese bamboo—not visible to the eye. It is certainly true that "a good many do not see it now [the Word of God], to take their position," but Ellen White reminds us that "these things are influencing their lives, and when the message goes with a loud voice they will be ready for it."[4]

Therefore, which prophecy must currently be fulfilled through the literature ministry? We are, as previously mentioned, currently in the eye of the hurricane of Revelation 7, and the work now underway is the sealing of God's people. That raises the question: Is the ministry of the printed page in some way related to the sealing of God's people during this time? If so, is the link merely peripheral, or is there a primary, decisive relationship between the two? Let's see what the Bible says.

Four angels announce the sealing

The prophet Ezekiel introduces the idea of the first sealing angel, who has in his hands the *instrument* that results in the sealing. The second angel, who appears in Revelation 7, tells us *the time* in the world's history when the sealing is to take place. The third angel, of Revelation 14, announces *the message* about the sealing that must go to all people of the world—our message. And finally, the fourth and sealing angel appears in Revelation 18. He possesses *the power* that consummates the sealing of God's own.

The sealing angel of Ezekiel 9: a sealing instrument

"He cried also in mine ears with a loud voice, saying, Cause them that have charge over the city to draw near, even every man with his destroying weapon in his hand. And, behold, six men came from the way of the higher gate, which lieth toward the north, and every man a slaughter weapon in his hand; and one man among them was clothed with linen, with a *writer's inkhorn* by his side: and they went in, and stood beside the brasen altar. And the glory of the God of Israel was gone up from the cherub, whereupon he was, to the threshold of the house. And he called to the man clothed with linen, which had *the writer's inkhorn* by his side; and the Lord said unto him, Go through the midst of the city, through the midst of Jerusalem, and set a mark upon the foreheads of the men that sigh and that cry for all the abominations that be done in the midst thereof. And to the others he said in mine hearing, Go ye after him through the city, and smite: let not your eye spare, neither have ye pity" (Eze. 9:1-5).

By analyzing Ezekiel 9, we learn that the Lord has ordered the sealing of His people before the destruction of the nation. Its function is to identify the faithful ones so that they will not be harmed during the impending destruction.

The text calls our attention to the fact that God has entrusted the sealing process to the evocative image of *an angel who carries with him something like stenographic equipment.* The Hebrew word *keset*, which the King James Version of the Bible translates as "the writer's inkhorn" (verse 2), is rendered in the New Living Translation as "a writer's case."

Unfortunately, we often overlook that the angel must use the written word to complete his mission. He is to put a mark on the foreheads of the chosen. What does it symbolize? The Hebrew uses the phrase *hitvita taw*, translated as "set a *taw* mark." William H. Shea notes that "in this particular example the use of the letter *taw* as a special marker may derive its importance from the fact that it was the last letter of the Hebrew alphabet. By demarcating individuals selected in this manner, the angel marked them as the *last* of the righteous, that is, the righteous *remnant* who were to be saved from the destruction to come upon Judah and Jerusalem."[5]

Therefore in his work of sealing, the angel must use both writing equipment as well as letters. Does this prophecy apply to our time?

The time of the first sealing angel

Ellen White described "angels hurrying to and fro in heaven. An angel with a writer's inkhorn by his side returned from the earth and reported to Jesus that his work was done, and the saints were numbered and sealed. Then I saw Jesus, who had been ministering before the ark containing the ten commandments, throw down the censer."[6]

If the foregoing had no connection with the three angels' messages, it would be rather insignificant. But here we find an allusion to the current work of sealing God's saints, the angel in charge, and the instrument he uses. According to the vision, the angel currently doing the sealing is one carrying writing equipment. In another statement relating to the last days, we read the following: "The angel with the writer's inkhorn *is to place a mark* upon the foreheads of all who are separated from sin and sinners, and the destroying angel follows this angel."[7]

In other words, to Ellen White, the work of sealing is in the hands of this angel whose mission *is something that is pending, but is currently under way*. As such, is this the same angel as the one brought to view in Revelation 7 and also pictured as completing a process of sealing?

The angel of Revelation 7: the timing of the sealing

"And after these things I saw four angels standing on the four corners of the earth, holding the four winds of the earth, that the wind should not blow on the earth, nor on the sea, nor on any tree. And I saw another angel ascending from the east, having the seal of the living God: and he cried with a loud voice to the four angels, to whom it was given to hurt the earth and the sea, saying, Hurt not the earth, neither the sea, nor the trees, till we have sealed the servants of our God in their foreheads" (Rev. 7:1-3).

Here again is the eye of the hurricane. First we notice that *the timing* of the sealing must come *between the sixth and seventh seal.* The sixth seal concerns *the signs* announcing Christ's impending return, and the seventh is *His actual return.*

The sealing, then, must occur after the darkening of the sun and moon, and the falling of the stars from heaven, which are the sixth seal (Rev. 6:12, 13), and just prior to the Second Coming, when "there was silence in heaven about the space of half an hour" (Rev. 8:1), which constitutes the seventh seal.

Now, on whom is the seal of God placed? Without question, here is one of the most interesting features of the prophecy. First of all, the 12 tribes of Israel no longer exist as such, which leads us to the following: Prophecies that did not see complete fulfillment in literal Israel but will apply to spiritual Israel.

Hans K. LaRondelle explains that "Revelation 7 needs to be understood as the worldwide antitype of the historical types in Exodus 12 and Ezekiel 9."[8] What was local in application is now cosmic and universal. Spiritual Israel is to be sealed, and among the means that the Lord will use to accomplish it is the angel with a writer's inkhorn—writing equipment that employs the written word to complete a mission.

Intimate link of the second to the first sealing angel

In *Testimonies to Ministers,* in respect to the sealing of Revelation 7, we read that "this sealing of the servants of God is the same that was shown to Ezekiel in vision. John also had been a witness of this most startling revelation."[9]

Ellen White's reference is to the sealing activity of the angel of Revelation 7, and she says that it was the same vision seen by the prophet Ezekiel. In stating that John also saw "the same," we are to understand that it is not a *new* sealing but the one that God intended for His people all along.

Therefore the fact that the sealing in Ezekiel and Revelation are one and the same can only mean that *the angel with the writer's inkhorn must be at work now,* and thus represents the sealing angel of the sixth and seventh seals. But who is the angel?

The sealing angel of Revelation 14: the message of the sealing

"And the third angel followed them, saying with a loud voice, If any man worship the beast and his image, and receive his mark in his forehead, or in his hand, the same shall drink of the wine of the wrath of God, which is poured out without mixture into the cup of his indignation; and he shall be tormented with fire and brimstone in the presence of the holy angels, and in the presence of the Lamb: and the smoke of their torment ascendeth up for ever and ever: and they have no rest day nor night, who worship the beast and his image, and whosoever receiveth the mark of his name. Here is the patience of the saints: here are they that keep the commandments of God, and the faith of Jesus" (Rev. 14:9-12).

The reasons for assigning sealing status to the third angel of Revelation 14 are the following: In the first place, *the third angel announces the truth about the Sabbath, a sealing truth.* His warning against worship of the beast or his image also suggests where to direct our worship. The seal of God is in the Sabbath (Eze. 20:12). Therefore the mark of the beast is a false day of worship. And given that it is an official teaching of the Seventh-day Adventist Church that Sunday will only be the mark of the beast in a future context,[10] it is our job to prepare the world by providing the necessary arguments that will enable many to choose for the right during what will be a terribly difficult time.

Second, *the timing of his appearance* identifies the third angel with the sealing angel of Revelation 7. The basis of this argument is simply that the sealing *is the last work* God will accomplish on behalf of humanity, which parallels the action of the third angel. And as the message of sealing leads to the actual sealing of a whole multitude, the result of the third angel's message is that a great multitude *obeys the commandments of God* and *has the faith of Jesus.* These ultimate expressions of loyalty are the truths that will mature the sealing.

The third angel compared to the second sealing angel

As Uriah Smith wrote: "The angel with the seal of the living God is therefore the same as the third angel of Revelation 14."[11] Does such a claim have a biblical foundation? Hans K. LaRondelle adds to this statement:

"The mission of this angel [the sealing angel of Revelation 7] anticipates that of the angel of Revelation 10 [fulfilled in the experience of the Adventists of 1844], which is unfolded further in the threefold message of Revelation 14:6-12" in the Adventist movement. In other words, "God will send a special message . . . *to secure a people*" who will remain faithful to God during the "hour of trial that is going to come on the whole world to test the inhabitnts of the earth" (Rev. 3:10, NIV).[12]

Ellen White also saw that the four angels would hold the winds "*until*

Jesus' work was done in the sanctuary,"[13] which implies that the sealing is simultaneous with the investigative judgment and with the ongoing message of the third angel:

"As the ministration of Jesus closed in the holy place, and He passed into the holiest, and stood *before the ark containing the law of God*, He *sent another mighty angel with a third message* to the world."[14]

Here, then, we find a startling parallelism: *investigative judgment, third angel's message, sealing.*

In explaining the sealing of Ezekiel 9, which is parallel to Revelation 7, William H. Shea observed that "the execution of the sentence [of the destroying angels among those not sealed] was the result of decisions reached *during the sessions of judgment* in the temple"[15]—that is, during the investigative judgment of Judah.

The identity of the sealing angel in Revelation 7

Who, then, is the sealing angel of Revelation 7? Clearly it represents the church whose work it is to proclaim the third angel's message. Ellen White tells us that "the nations will be angry, yet held in check so as *not to prevent the work of the third angel.*"[16] Notice that according to the quote, the four angels restrain events to facilitate the work of the sealing angel of Revelation 14:9 and *not* that of the sealing angel of Revelation 7, though in the context of our study both are one and the same.

When Ellen White wrote of a train going at great speed, whose conductor was Satan, it appeared to her that the whole world was on board, for which reason she asked the angel the whereabouts of God's people. The angel bid her look in the other direction, and there she saw two groups appearing to be bound up into bundles, or companies. Then the angel explained that "the third angel is *binding*, or *sealing*, them in bundles for the heavenly garner."[17] According to this statement, who is the sealing angel? It is the third angel.

Later on, in the same book, we can read further:

"I then saw *the third angel*. Said my accompanying angel, 'Fearful is his work. Awful is his mission. He is the angel that is to select the wheat from the tares, and seal, or *bind*, the wheat for the heavenly garner.'"[18]

As such, the sealing angel is currently the third angel.

The sealing: what it is and how it happens

Now, in order to explain how the sealing takes place and why the printed page is intimately involved, first we have to understand *what* the sealing is. It is "not any seal or mark that can be seen, but *a settling into the truth*, both *intellectually and spiritually*, so they cannot be moved."[19] But what does that mean? Just this: To the extent that our publications have power to lead people into truth both intellectually and spiritually, they can bring about the sealing. It is in every sense, then, that we can rightly call our publications prophets of the sealing.

Let me give you an illustration. A dictionary defines the word "character" as "a spiritual sign remaining in a person as a result of *knowledge or experience deemed important.*" It further applies this same term to a "*sign or mark that is printed*, painted or sculpted," and extends it to "*a sign of writing or printing.*" As if that were not enough, it says that it is "a brand or iron with which animals from of one flock are *distinguished from those of another.*"[20] Interestingly, even a dictionary definition links the sealing to the press.

The reason I highlight the link between character and the sealing is that the seal received by the 144,000 is also a *written* name,[21] and the name of the sealed is based on their character.[22] The antitype (Rev. 7; 14) finds a link to the type (Eze. 9). The prophet Ezekiel indicated that the work of the sealing must go forth by divine fiat with a writer's inkhorn that employs the written word in the accomplishment of its mission.

Therefore the argument behind the proposition that the publications bearing the truth are *in verity* the prophets of the sealing is as follows: The work of the angel with the writer's inkhorn *is currently in force* and the spiritual and intellectual settling into truth is predicted to take place through our publishing houses. It is that simple. Its opposite, the mark of the beast, is a growing acceptance of deception.

This may have been the reason that Ellen White stated most emphatically, "God has ordained the canvassing work as a means of presenting before the people the light contained in our books, and canvassers should be impressed with the importance of bringing before the world as fast as possible the books necessary for their spiritual education and enlightenment. *This is the very work the Lord would have His people do at this time.* All who consecrate themselves to God to work as canvassers are assisting to give the last message of warning to the world."[23] Through the books they distribute, they are presenting the sealing message.

The 1848 vision: the sealing and publishing

When Ellen G. White received a vision on the need for publishing, she wrote the following:

"At a meeting held in Dorchester, Massachusetts, November, 1848, I had been given a view . . ."

A view of what? We read further:

". . . *a view of the proclamation of the sealing message,* and of the duty of the brethren to publish the light that was shining upon our pathway. After coming out of vision, I said to my husband: 'I have a message for you. *You must begin to print.*'"[24]

Notice that God founded the publishing program with a specific object in view: *to proclaim the message of the sealing.* A decisive evangelistic mission, if faithfully carried out, fulfills a prophecy. And it is something that God has called the church as a whole to fulfill.

While it is true that God is currently employing other media to carry on this sacred work, the inspired counsel warns us:

"Let it never be forgotten that these institutions [printing presses] are to cooperate with the ministry of the delegates of heaven. They are among the agencies *represented by the angel flying* 'in the midst of heaven, having the everlasting gospel.'"[25]

When the members of our churches distribute material containing such decisive truths, they are helping to fulfill the prophecy of the sealing—and you can do the same thing! Every believer thus becomes the angel with the writer's inkhorn to "settle people into the truth both intellectually and spiritually." That is why Ellen White declares that "there is no higher work than evangelistic canvassing, for it *involves the performance of the highest moral duties.*"[26]

Recognizing that it is a blessing to have literature evangelists in our churches, we should rightly esteem their work and pray for them. In addition, what a great blessing it is whenever anyone expends large sums to distribute the message through handing out books.

As a student literature evangelist I personally always felt that I was doing something important, yet I never imagined it to be the overarching work it truly is. And that is not all; we must examine one other matter: What is the function of the fourth sealing angel, and at what time does he appear?

The sealing angel of Revelation 18: power to complete the sealing work

"And after these things I saw another angel come down from heaven, having great power; and the earth was lightened with his glory. And he cried mightily with a strong voice, saying, Babylon the great is fallen, is fallen, and is become the habitation of devils, and the hold of every foul spirit, and a cage of every unclean and hateful bird. . . . And I heard another voice from heaven, saying, Come out of her, my people, that ye be not partakers of her sins, and that ye receive not of her plagues" (Rev. 18:1-4).

Many Adventist publishing leaders have considered the angel of Revelation as the angel of publishing. They base it on Ellen White's 1902 statement:

"In a large degree through *our publishing houses* is to be accomplished the work of that other angel who comes down from heaven with great power, and who lightens the earth with his glory."[27]

Yet such a view requires some correction. When we apply the role of "that other angel" exclusively to publishing, we forget that the church has other departments that the angel will also use as he lightens the world. Notice that Ellen White states "in a large degree"—that is, not exclusively— but *also through* this medium (our publishing houses) will the work of Revelation 18's angel be completed.

Satellite evangelism, small groups, one-on-one Bible studies in homes, radio, television, and the Internet are among very powerful media that God is using now, in this time, to enlighten the world. However, the significance of publishing lies in that it will go on proclaiming truth when the use of other media will have been made extremely difficult. As stated already, *it is much easier to ban a broadcast than to confiscate books already in the hands of the masses.*

All of this hints that the angel of Revelation 18 must represent something else. That may explain why Ellen White advises that "God's people are to understand in regard to the angel who is to lighten the whole world with his glory, while he cries mightily with a loud voice: 'Babylon the great is fallen, is fallen.'"[28]

The identity of the angel of Revelation 18

We find ourselves, then, with the need to identify this powerful angel. By doing so, we will gain another clue to understanding why we can consider the books containing the last-day message as *prophets of the sealing.*

I will not go into great detail here, but will limit discussion to "this is the power of the latter rain of the Holy Spirit."[29] In His prophetic sermon Jesus warned us about false christs and false prophets who will "show great signs and wonders to deceive, if possible" (Matt. 24:24, NKJV). But God will not leave the world in darkness. The world will be enlightened at the time of the end with the glory of a being of divine origin so that humanity may not be deceived. What's more, the Holy Spirit will work miracles that will far outweigh the enemy's efforts.

Remember what happened with Moses and Aaron in Egypt. The Bible says that "the rod of Aaron devoured" that of the enemies.[30] In the last days God will provide a superior manifestation of His divine power that overawes that of His enemies, all with the purpose of inviting His people to come, not now out of Egypt, but out of Babylon (cf. Ex. 7:1-12).

Just as supernatural power accompanied the preaching of Noah to give his message credence, in the same way the message of the third angel will have Holy Spirit power:

"But as the days of [Noah] were, so shall also the coming of the Son of man be" (Matt. 24:37).

God did not depend solely upon Noah's preaching. Through the animals entering the ark in an orderly fashion, the Spirit spoke to the consciences of the people. It was a special message with a special demonstration of supernatural, divine power. As it turns out, Ellen White, too, equates the angel of Revelation 18 with the Holy Spirit in latter-rain power:

"I have no specific time of which to speak when *the outpouring of the Holy Spirit* will take place—when the mighty angel will come down from heaven *and unite with the third angel* in closing up the work for this world."[31]

Later on she stated: "It is with an earnest longing that I look forward to the time *when the events of the Day of Pentecost shall be repeated* with even greater power than on that occasion. John says, 'I saw another angel come down from heaven, having great power; and the earth was lightened with his glory.'"[32]

Notice the direct link she makes between the angel of Revelation 18:1 and the day of Pentecost. Unquestionably it is a reference to the pouring out of the Holy Spirit.

In still another place she adds: "The great outpouring of the Spirit of God, which lightens the whole earth with His glory, will not come until we have an enlightened people, that know by experience what it means to be laborers together with God."[33]

When will the people of God be ready to cooperate in His work in unity of spirit? I would like to suggest that, having access to the printed page, we can all act a part. As Gilson Grudtner so ably put it: "This is the best method to involve the majority of [church] members in fulfilling the church's mission."[34] In just three years his church alone has distributed more than 60,000 silent messengers, uniting itself with the work of the sealing angel.

The sealing in plural: until we have sealed

Another point we should not ignore is that the angel of Revelation 18, or the Holy Spirit, *also* represents the sealing angel of Revelation 7, in completing the *divine phase* of the sealing work. Therefore if the sealing angel of Revelation 7 is the third angel, we can also view Him as a member of the Godhead. It must be so in view of the fact that *we cannot say that it is the church who orders the angels to hold or release the winds.* Rather, it is something that only God can do.[35]

Further, Paul stated that one of the roles of the Holy Spirit is to seal the people of God: "After that ye believed, ye were sealed with that holy Spirit" (Eph. 1:13).

"Grieve not the holy Spirit of God, whereby ye are sealed unto the day of redemption" (Eph. 4:30).

Of course, the foregoing does not remove the church from participating in the sealing work. As C. Mervyn Maxwell points out: "The three angels of Revelation 14, *even the sealing angel* of chapter 7, represent Christians *entrusted with God's message.*"[36]

In fact, Revelation 7:3 mentions a sealing involving various forces. We don't hear the sealing angel state, "Hold back the winds until I have sealed," but rather "until *we* [plural] have sealed the servants of our God on their foreheads." For this reason I suggest that the expression "we" refers as much to the Holy Spirit as it does the church. In the context of the last days it is the Spirit and the bride (the church) who say, "Come" (Rev. 22:17).

The sealing work contains both a human element that we as a church must carry out and a divine aspect that we cannot fulfill. In 1897 Ellen White wrote, "By the work of the Holy Spirit *the truth is riveted in the mind and printed in the heart* of the diligent, God-fearing student."[37]

The great urgency: distribution of the message in our time

But many ask if it is truly imperative that we distribute books right now. LaRondelle answers this question:

"Only by uniting Revelation 17 and 18 do we become aware of the urgency and timeliness of the final warning message."

"While chapter 17 reveals Satan's final grasp for world dominion through the beast which '*will come up out of the Abyss*' (17:8, NIV), in chapter 18 God acts through the angel who *comes down from heaven* with great authority (18:1, NIV)."[38]

So while one *ascends*, the other *comes down*. Who gets there first? God will act through that angel who will use the printing presses to enlighten the world *before it shall be forever too late.*

Woe to those who block or discourage such a prophetic work

So the sealing is a "settling into the truth." By virtue of being of an intellectual character it is carried out by the angel with a writer's inkhorn, who must place his seal using the written word and by extension, printed books, an "instrument" of writing. As we have seen, the angel is currently at work and represents the angels in Revelation 7 and 14:9. Between them they depict the human phase of the sealing process. The first one bears the instrument, the second provides the timing, and the third presents the message that produces the sealing.

But since the sealing is also of a spiritual nature, the angel of Revelation 18, who symbolizes the Holy Spirit in latter-rain power, depicts the divine phase of the sealing. This angel unites with the third angel's preaching to bring about the loud cry and uses the printing press to complete His work.

In conclusion, then, the publishing program has a prophetic nature. It is God-ordained and, as such, will see ultimate success. Thus its role is a prominent one, sanctioned by the Holy Spirit. Those who have a part in it will cooperate with God in saving countless people. What could be more important than the work of sealing those who will be heirs with Christ throughout eternity? In chapter 6 we will explore additional details concerning the sealing: the 144,000 and the great multitude.

For all the reasons outlined so far we believe the church's publishing program is not merely the result of human doing. God has created all things. Ultimately it is to Him that we must render an account of what we did with this sacred ministry.

A solemn call

The only way to save the world from deadly end-time deceptions is by *sealing* it. Whoever does not receive the seal of God will have the mark of the beast and will receive the seven last plagues. Will God not therefore hold us responsible if we fail to warn the world of the overpowering delusions at the end-time?

Herbert Douglass wonders, "How will we ever face up to reality when we realize that we knew something about the future that we could have made clearer to our children, to our neighbors, to men and women everywhere—but we neglected this privilege and duty?"[39] And Marvin Moore states, "Suppose that I had absolutely certain information that sometime in the next five years your house would burn to the ground—however, I couldn't give you a date; it might be any time during those five years. How would you want me to relate this information? I might hesitate to warn you of the impending danger, because you'd think my prediction was foolish. Which would you prefer—that I not tell you in order to avoid looking stupid or that I tell you and let you decide how to relate to the information? That's the issue Seventh-day Adventist have faced for 150 years."[40]

Now, if we believe that God Himself has entrusted us with preaching the gospel to the world in the last days, then we should take the matter seriously, because "no other people have a clearer map for the road ahead. No other people have been given the responsibility of sharing the truth about the future with others."[41]

We are "not to engage in work that will hinder" us from distributing Seventh-day Adventist literature. Though "*some injudicious minister*"[42] may hinder it, we are still to press it forward. Woe to those who discourage individuals who have decided to become literature evangelists! It is a ministry born in the mind of God, and He has communicated it to His church to preach the gospel and so contribute to the work of the sealing.[43]

Recently General Conference president Ted Wilson shared the following:

"Here is a question I have been asked: 'Elder Wilson, as we look to the new quinquennium, what is your vision for the publishing arm of the work?' In other words, do you have a dream for the publishing ministry's future? I'd like to answer that question with a resounding 'yes!' My dream for the publishing ministry is alive and well. It is basically simple, yet exceedingly large. It is simple because it involves just three key words, namely: *revival, reformation,* and *evangelism*. It is large because from these three words can evolve the greatest explosion of evangelistic progress through the print ministry that our world church has ever witnessed."[44]

With this in mind, I wonder: *Will we give publishing its rightful place? Will we make of it what God proposes to accomplish through it? What kind of effort would the worldwide membership invest in it if they realized they were fulfilling a most solemn prophecy? What would happen if all the literature evangelists understood its importance?* The books, magazines, and magabooks distributed today are preparing the world stage for the Holy Spirit to manifest His glorious power. Will you play a part in this?

The sown seed is about to bear much fruit. But when? Turn the page.

---

[1] E. G. White, *Colporteur Ministry*, p. 11. (Italics supplied.)

[2] "Apostolic Letter *Dies Domini* by the Holy Father John Paul II to the Bishops, Clergy, and Faithful on the Sanctification of Sunday," at www.vatican.va/holy_father/john_paul_ii/apost_letters/documents/hf_jp-ii_apl_05071998_dies-domini_en.html.

[3] E. G. White, *Colporteur Ministry*, p. 128. (Italics supplied.)

[4] E. G. White, *Last Day Events,* pp. 212, 213.

[5] William H. Shea, *Selected Studies on Prophetic Interpretation* (Silver Spring, Md.: General Conference of Seventh-day Adventists, 1982), p. 16.

[6] E. G. White, *Early Writings*, p. 279.

[7] *The Seventh-day Adventist Bible Commentary,* Ellen G. White Comments, vol. 4, p. 1161. (Italics supplied.)

[8] H. K. LaRondelle. *How to Understand the End-Time Prophecies of the Bible*, p. 153.

[9] Ellen G. White, *Testimonies to Ministers* (Mountain View, Calif.: Pacific Press Pub. Assn, 1923), p. 445.

[10] See *Seventh-day Adventists Answer Questions on Doctrine* (Washington, D.C.: Review and Herald Pub. Assn., 1957), p. 181.

[11] Uriah Smith, *The Prophecies of Daniel and the Revelation,* rev. ed. (Nashville: Southern Pub. Assn., 1944), p. 462.

[12] LaRondelle, p. 151.

[13] E. G. White, *Early Writings*, p. 36. (Italics supplied.)

[14] *Ibid.*, p. 254. (Italics supplied.)

[15] Shea, p. 17. (Italics supplied.)

[16] E. G. White, *Early Writings*, p. 85. (Italics supplied.)

[17] *Ibid.*, p. 88. (Italics supplied.)

[18] *Ibid.*, p. 118. (Italics supplied.) "Adventists have generally held that the sealing angel of Revelation 7:2-3, who seals God's end-time people (while other angelic forces hold back the winds of total trouble and strife), is to be identified with the work of the third angel of Revelation 14:9-11" (Beatrice S. Neall, "Sealed Saints and the Tribulation," *Symposium on Revelation,* book 1, p. 245).

[19] E. G. White, *Last Day Events*, p. 219. (Italics supplied.)

[20] http://lema.rae.es/drae/?val=carácter.

[21] E. G. White, *Last Day Events*, p. 223.

[22] C. Mervyn Maxwell, *God Cares: The Message of Revelation* (Boise, Idaho: Pacific Press Pub. Assn., 1985), vol. 2, p. 384.

[23] E. G. White, *Testimonies for the Church*, vol. 6, p. 313. (Italics supplied.)

[24] E. G. White, *Colporteur Ministry,* p. 1. (Italics supplied.)

[25] Ellen G. White, *Counsels to Writers and Editors* (Nashville: Southern Pub. Assn., 1946), p. 179. (Italics supplied.)

[26] E. G. White, *Testimonies*, vol. 6, p. 331. (Italics supplied.)

[27] E. G. White, *Christian Service*, p. 148. (Italics supplied.)

[28] *The Seventh-day Adventist Bible Commentary,* Ellen G. White Comments, vol. 7, p. 985.

[29] M. Veloso, *Apocalipsis y el Fin del Mundo* [*Revelation and the End of the World*], p. 185.

[30] See Loron Wade, *El Futuro del Mundo Revelado en Apocalipsis* [*The World's Future*

Revealed in Revelation] (Colombia: Asociación Publicadora Interamericana, 1987), pp. 217-221.

[31] E. G. White, *Last Day Events,* pp. 194, 195. (Italics supplied.)

[32] *Ibid.,* p. 202. (Italics supplied.)

[33] E. G. White, *Christian Service,* p. 253.

[34] In Almir Marroni, "Interview With a Church Pastor," *The Literature Evangelist,* April-September 2007, p. 31.

[35] E. G. White, *Testimonies to Ministers,* pp. 445, 446.

[36] Maxwell, *God Cares,* vol. 2, p. 463. (Italics supplied.)

[37] *The Seventh-day Adventist Bible Commentary,* Ellen G. White Comments, vol. 5, pp. 1147, 1148. (Italics supplied.)

[38] LaRondelle, p. 421.

[39] Herbert E. Douglass. *Dramatic Prophecies of Ellen White: Stories of World Events Divinely Foretold* (Nampa, Idaho: Pacific Press Pub. Assn., 2007), p. 134.

[40] Marvin Moore, *Could It Really Happen?* (Nampa, Idaho: Pacific Press Pub. Assn., 2008), p. 264.

[41] Douglass, p. 134.

[42] E. G. White, *Colporteur Ministry,* pp. 24, 28. (Italics supplied.)

[43] Much of this chapter first appeared as part of the Sabbath school materials in the magazine *Avanzad* under the title: "The Prophets of the Sealing Are Here Now: *You Can Cooperate With Them!*" 2nd trimester 2008.

[44] *The Literature Evangelist,* January-March 2011, p. 9.

Chapter 4

Prophets That Speak in the Wilderness

An ancient prophecy foretold that at the end-time *one book would be read*, and so it happened. God announced to Daniel that his book would be sealed till the time of the end (Dan. 12:4), and centuries later, during the Millerite movement, the book was opened *to do its work as prophesied* (Rev. 10:2-11). God spoke, and it was so. The sealed book was read, and a powerful spiritual revival arose. Was it a type of what our publications will accomplish in the final days?

A documentary on deserts declares that "Death Valley is the most embracing place on earth."[1] Then, after a string of images showing the desolation caused by drought, the narrator continues with a triumphant tone: "Even this oven can be transformed by water!" The DVD then cuts to scenes of millions of flowers covering the arid desert. "A simple downpour can cause seeds that slept for 30 years or more to come alive again." The program ends with a sense of quiet awe as the narrator announces, "And there has not been a flowering like this in over a century!"[2]

The Bible presents something very similar in connection with what we have outlined in this book: *the printed page at the end of time*.

The desert about to turn into a fruitful field

The prophet Isaiah saw our day in vision when he said, "Is it not yet a very little while, and Lebanon shall be turned into a fruitful field, and the fruitful field shall be esteemed as a forest?" (Isa. 29:17).

To begin with, two things need to happen for a desert to become a fruitful field. First, abundant rain. Second, a lot of seed in the ground. Nothing will happen without both being present. However, if both conditions appear in a field, the transformation is inevitable.

I want to suggest that the words in Isaiah 29 will apply to our imminent future. First, the context certainly indicates the time of the end. The passage says that the violent one "is brought to nought, and *the scorner is consumed*" (verse 20), something that we know has yet to happen. Of course, it is undeniable that the prophecy had a partial fulfillment in the person of Sennacherib in Hezekiah's time,[3] but a more complete fulfillment will take place at the destruction of the earth.

Second, Isaiah records the fact that this will not happen "until the spirit be poured upon us from on high" (Isa. 32:15). Then will the desert turn into a fruitful field, and the fruitful field be regarded as a forest. It is because the outpouring of the Holy Spirit has yet to happen that we can safely conclude that the prophecy has a future application. Though the Spirit was poured out on the day of Pentecost, we have yet to see the latter rain in the time of the end, "before the great and the terrible day of the Lord" (Joel 2:31).

Some scholars foresee the day that, according to Isaiah 32:15, "the time would come when there would be *outpourings* of God's Spirit *upon the world*, which would cause regions spiritually *barren and desolate* to bloom as the rose."[4]

Is there a link to literature in all this? Isaiah wrote, "In that day shall the deaf hear the words of the book" (Isa. 29:18). Notice that, according to the prophecy, the deaf shall hear not the words of a person, but those *of the book*. It is in this sense that the desert shall become a fruitful field, and those seeds scattered so widely will "spring up among weeds" all around the world.

In truth, it is impossible to count the high number of seeds that can lie in a fallow field. People living in rural areas recognize that after the rainy season the desert truly can become a fertile zone. When no rain falls, the seeds are not visible to the naked eye; but once the monsoons come, the picture changes drastically. Rain turns the desert into a sea of green.

Today we see only a vast spiritual desert of enormous cities, apparently unreachable. But we hardly suspect the great quantity of seed—millions and millions of printed pages scattered all around the world, containing the message and awaiting a single event to sprout: for the Spirit to be poured out from on high. Once that happens, "more than one thousand will soon be converted in one day, most of whom will trace their first convictions to the reading of our publications."[5]

Such an interpretation is diametrically opposed to a Mormon interpretation,[6] claiming that the "book" to which Isaiah refers—which the deaf would hear in the last days—is the *Book of Mormon*.[7]

Interestingly, Mormons interpret the conversion of the desert into a fruitful field as brought about after literal rains that happened in Lebanon from 1842 to 1845. Given that the *Book of Mormon* first appeared in 1830, they say, "If that book is not the *Book of Mormon*, then which book is it? The latter rains have fallen in Lebanon, and it has become fertile. Therefore the book referred to in this prophecy must be here now."[8]

Notwithstanding, Isaiah is not speaking of "new light," as they claim, but is merely referring to the powerful means that God will use to reach the world. It talks about a sowing and rain, but the rain is the Holy Spirit, and the seed is, I believe, each and every book containing the last-day message.

But is there a guarantee anyone will actually read the books, when today hardly anyone even glances at a page? Remember, God predicted that the time would come when people would read and understand the prophecies of Daniel. God always uses simple methods to carry out His purposes.

The power of the media versus the power of the gospel

Since 1946 Editorial Vida has solidified itself as the leader of evangelistic publications in Spanish. As a worldwide ministry of the Assemblies of God Church it considers that the printed page "is an answer that will give the truth to the world's 3 billion unreached people."[9]

According to Bill L. Williams, president of Life Publishers International in Eastern Europe and Russia, "Christian literature is one of the salient tools God is using to reach people with the gospel and revitalize believers. We believe that the work of publishing the truth of God is vital for the growth of the church. *We believe in the power of the printed page to transform hearts and lead men to be reconciled to God.*"

Bob Hoskins, one-time director of that ministry, says, "I am 100 percent convinced that through mass distribution of the Book God has placed in our hands, we can snatch millions from the burning who will rise up at that judgment day to call us *blessed.*"[10] His book, itself an adaptation of the four Gospels (entitled *Book of Hope*), has a distribution of more than 700 million in 80 languages and more than 125 countries,[11] and is targeted to children and youth.

"Down through history, God has used the written word to give His message to the world," he continues. "I am awed to realize the importance of *books* in all of these end-time events." Moreover, "when the mighty angel appeared in the vision of John, the main instrument of his power was a little book [see Rev. 10:2]. . . . In his hand, as the main instrument of his power, he held 'a little book open.'"[12]

Is this angel pointing out the method we should use to take the gospel to the world, as in the multitudes referred to by Scripture (Rev. 10:2; see

Rev. 17:15)? Recall that this is the same angel who issued the order to prophesy again (Rev. 10:11), something that happened before and after 1844, chiefly through means of the printed page.[13]

And although Carmelo Martines warns us against confusing resources with methods and places literature in the resources category,[14] the truth of the matter is that Ellen G. White calls literature a method and categorizes it as second to none.[15] And although a book does not fill the requirement of being a disciple, as Martines' research calls for—since it is not a thinking, learning person—we must recognize that the printed page, once placed in the homes, becomes a preacher and an evangelist.[16] The most awe-inspiring aspect of this fact is that books fulfill a prophecy by participating in the sealing work, and they do so without the presence of a living person.

Hoskins further explains, "The power of the gospel is not in a building. It is not in a man. *The power of gospel is in the gospel!* The gospel *is* the power of God unto salvation!"[17] Dick Eastman reasons that the gospel *doesn't even need to be voiced* to have an impact.[18] In truth, the message of the gospel is "good news" independently, regardless of the form of delivery.

This means that if we do not believe in the methods that God uses, as insignificant as they may appear to be, it is because we have not been convinced of *the power of the gospel*. We make a mistake if we attribute the power to the agency employed rather than to the message itself. It is one of the biggest errors we can fall into when considering how to complete the presentation of the gospel to the world.

Even "trash" has the power to save

I have in my hands a copy of the January 1976 issue of the magazine *El Centinela*. The cover is shredded, but one can still notice that it is Special Issue No. 80. Inside, the editors explain that it had a printing of 800,000 and a projected readership of 2 million.

The back cover is missing because the owner removed it when she noticed it in front of her home, lying in mud. But after 30 years the contents are still intact. And its pages tell a larger story of salvation.

When Guadalupe Pérez found the magazine, she at first picked it up to place it in a wastepaper basket. She walked into her home and laid it aside while she went to retrieve the basket. Little did she realize the treasure she had just brought into her home. It was a message the Lord Himself had mercifully brought to her door.

Since she had no intention of reading it, some hours passed before she came back to pick it up and toss it. But the Holy Spirit was present to prevent the Word from returning empty. Guadalupe began to wonder what was in the magazine.

As she leafed through the pages the articles seemed interesting: "Who Are Adventists?"; "Why Do Adventists Observe the Sabbath?"; "What Do Seventh-day Adventists Believe?"; "The Gospel to the World"; "How to Have a Happy and Harmonious Family"; "There Is Hope"; "How to Live Healthy."

As her eyes traced the lines on the dusty pages the door of her heart started to open. She became so interested that she asked her husband, "Where is the church that published this magazine?" He, being a taxi driver, recalled that a pastor at the University of Navojoa would regularly hand him leaflets with the word "Adventist." They phoned the school and found out that, yes, there was a church nearby. Today she is a member of the Seventh-day Adventist Church.

How do such things happen? Guadalupe assumed that her neighbor, an ardent Catholic, must have tossed it out as he did other Protestant publications. But because the Lord's endeavors always succeed, a muddy magazine entitled "A Christian Ideal for Humanity" became a powerful illustration of one of the most simple and far-reaching ways to evangelize the world.

The church's most far-reaching evangelistic project

To get an idea of what this means, we need only consider that our own world church is currently in the middle of the largest effort ever undertaken to distribute the book *The Great Controversy*. Ted Wilson, General Conference president, says it is his "firm conviction . . . that there will be thousands and thousands of highly committed Christians who will become [church] members through the Great Controversy Project and their contact with Seventh-day Adventist believers."[19]

Howard Faigao, publishing ministries director for the General Conference, adds, "We believe that we are living in the end-time of earth's history. Unprecedented world happenings are now pointing to Jesus' soon return. If the work of that other Angel of Revelation 18:1 is to be accomplished in a large degree by the circulation of our publications, then it is time for the church to distribute truth-filled literature as never before."[20]

"After the Bible, no other book has helped to win more souls than *The Great Controversy*," agrees Wilmar Hirle, associate publishing director of the General Conference. "Why? Because no other book speaks so clearly about Babylon as this one. When those who are in Babylon understand that this place is not as safe as they think, they [will] accept the invitation from God and come out of it. Herein lies the urgency of the message of *The Great Controversy*."[21]

Wilmar's statements fall right in line with Ellen White's own viewpoint:

"*The Great Controversy* should be very widely circulated. It contains the story of the past, the present, and the future. In its outline of the closing scenes of this earth's history, it bears a powerful testimony in behalf of the truth. I am more anxious to see a wide circulation for this book than for any others I have written; for in *The Great Controversy,* the last message of warning to the world is given more distinctly than in any of my other books."[22]

Can we ignore this unprecedented effort at thundering the loud cry? And is it really possible to reach a large part of the world with this method?

The mystery in the mighty mustard seed

The multitude that listened to Christ's teaching included many Pharisees. They noted contemptuously how few of His hearers acknowledged Him as the Messiah, and they questioned among themselves how such an unpretentious teacher could exalt Israel to universal dominion. Without riches, power, or honor, how was He to establish the new kingdom? Christ read their thoughts and answered them:

"'Whereunto shall we liken the kingdom of God? or with what comparison shall we compare it?' . . . 'It is like a grain of mustard seed,' He said, 'which, when it is sown upon the earth, though it be less than all the seeds that are upon the earth, yet when it is sown, groweth up, and becometh greater than all the herbs, and putteth out great branches; so that the birds of the heaven can lodge under the shadow thereof' (R.V.)."[23]

We notice that Jesus gave His parable in response to the doubts of the Pharisees concerning *how the universal kingdom of Christ was to be established*. They could not conceive how an unpopular rabbi, surrounded by 12 unlearned men, without riches or social status, could hope to have dominion. The mustard seed—something the Pharisees in that small group knew about—would serve as the symbol to illustrate His kingdom.

"Not only is the growth of Christ's kingdom illustrated by the parable of the mustard seed," Ellen White wrote, "but in every stage of its growth *the experience represented in the parable is repeated.* For His church in every generation *God has a special truth and a special work.*"[24]

According to her statement the development of the kingdom of God has various steps. And at every one the experience represented in the parable will repeat itself—that is, each stage will be small at the beginning but great at its point of full maturity. Jesus said that the kingdom of heaven "is like to a grain of mustard seed, which a man took, and sowed in his field: which indeed is the least of all seeds: but when it is grown, it is the greatest among herbs, and becometh a tree, so that the birds of the air come and lodge in the branches thereof" (Matt. 13:31, 32).

One of the more revealing aspects of the parable teaches that just as God has a special *truth* for every generation, He also has a special *work for His church* in that generation. Here is something we can easily and widely apply to our publishing program, given that it fits the principle taught in the parable.

One of Ellen White's inspired experiences expounds upon this principle:

"After coming out of vision, I said to my husband: 'I have a message for you. You must begin to print *a little paper* and send it out to the people. Let it be *small at first*; but as the people read, they will send you means with which to print, *and it will be a success from the first. From this small beginning* it was shown to me to be like streams of light that went clear round the world.' "[25]

It is not insignificant that as the mustard seed is tiny at first but then grows tremendously, so also has our publishing program. Truly we can apply the words in Job 8:7 to it: "Though thy beginning was small, yet thy latter end should greatly increase." And we are advised that *"this is the very work the Lord would have His people do at this time."*[26]

We know that the special truth for our time is the message of the three angels. And we must each personally recognize that, when it comes to the special work the church is to do at this time, literature evangelism dovetails with the prophecy. Along these lines, Ruth Ure offers these words of motivation:

"Evangelism, the foremost mission of the church, finds no more effective key than the printed word—primarily the Bible and secondarily *all* books which draw the reader by whatever path to think about God."[27]

Returning to the mustard seed concept, Ellen White foresaw that "in this last generation the parable of the mustard seed is to reach a signal and triumphant fulfillment. The little seed will become a tree. The last message of warning and mercy is to go to 'every nation and kindred and tongue'

(Rev. 14:6-14), 'to take out of them a people for his name' (Acts 15:14; Rev. 18:1). And the earth shall be lightened with His glory."[28]

But the question remains in many minds: *Can the publishing ministry really make a difference when people have little interest in religious materials?* Note that when God has stated that many will read, we must trust that they will do so:

"It is true that some who buy the books will lay them on the shelf or place them on the parlor table and seldom look at them. Still God has a care for His truth, and the time will come when these books will be sought for and read."[29]

It is written. Therefore, do not fret.

New circumstances bring new readers

"A good many do not see it now, to take their position, but these things are influencing their lives, and when the message goes with a loud voice they will be ready for it. They will not hesitate long; they will come out and take their position."[30]

The previous statement indicates that many people have not made a decision because circumstances are not currently what they should be. They will choose when the message goes forth with a loud cry. And when will that happen? When the Holy Spirit is poured out on God's people. It will take place when the Sabbath/Sunday controversy will be news around the world.

At that decisive crisis, books will play a decisive role. For example, as we previously noted: "The results of the circulation of this book [*The Great Controversy*] are not to be judged by what now appears. By reading it, some souls will be aroused, and will have courage to unite themselves at once with those who keep the commandments of God. But a much larger number who read it will not take their position *until they see the very events taking place that are foretold in it*."[31] And she informs us that it will occur at the final moments.

"But as the question of enforcing Sunday observance is widely agitated, the event so long doubted and disbelieved is seen to be approaching, and the third message will produce an effect which *it could not have had before*."[32]

Were you aware that this has happened previously in our church's history?

George R. Knight points out that prior to 1844, Miller's followers remained within their respective churches. "It was one thing to preach

Miller's 1843 message when it was some years off. But it was *quite another thing when the time approached*. A message that seemed harmless enough in the late 1830s threatened to disrupt the churches as the predicted year of the end of the world loomed on the horizon. As the predicted time came close, neutrality in the churches became an impossibility: *one had to either accept Millerism or reject it.*"[33]

And this same experience will repeat itself at the end with the Sabbath message.

Can we reject the message yet remain true?

Let's examine this statement: "The Lord has His representatives in all the churches. *These persons have not had the special testing truths* for these last days presented to them under circumstances that brought conviction to heart and mind; *therefore they have not, by rejecting light, severed their connection with God.*"[34]

Did you notice the apparent discrepancy? Depending on how we interpret the statement, it appears to say, on the one hand, that such individuals *have rejected light*, and on the other, that *they have not had the special testing truths* for the last days presented to them. Yet when we expected the statement to affirm that, *by rejecting light, they* have *severed their connection with God,* we find that such a thing has not happened. How can that be? After all, how is it possible to reject light not yet presented? On the other hand, how is it possible to maintain a relationship to God—not to sever the connection—even when rejecting light?[35]

The key to understanding such an apparent contradiction lies in the fact that the special testing truths for the last days have not yet come to them in a way that brings "conviction to heart and mind." That is the point. And it leads to this: Is the mark of the beast, especially the no-buy, no-sell mandate, a circumstance that will bring conviction to heart and mind? Certainly. Such conditions will cause people to remember what they read in our publications and will lead them to reconsider our message. But there is more.

Unusual circumstances unshackle

Ellen White revealed that the circumstances surrounding the death of Christ prepared the people to accept the gospel when confronted with the apostles' preaching.[36] The three hours of darkness around the cross, the earthquake, the veil rent in the Temple, the resurrection of the dead, etc., were enough to awaken conviction in the minds and hearts of the Jews of that time. *They were extraordinary happenings at an extraordinary moment.* Combined with the preaching in tongues on the day of Pentecost, many accepted the gospel. Circumstances, then, changed the hearts of the people.

It is said that hardship and trial reveal character. And in the trying circumstances that the people of the world will soon have to endure, what decisions will they make when opposed by the members of their own home? Where will our distributed publications be on that day, and what role will they play?

"The message will be carried not so much by argument as by the deep conviction of the Spirit of God. *The arguments have been presented.* The seed has been sown, and now it will spring up and bear fruit. *The publications distributed by missionary workers have exerted their influence,* yet many whose minds were impressed *have been prevented from fully comprehending the truth or from yielding obedience.* Now the rays of light penetrate everywhere, the truth is seen in its clearness, and the honest children of God sever the bands which have held them. Family connections, church relations, are *powerless to stay them now.* Truth is more precious than all besides. Notwithstanding the agencies combined against the truth, *a large number take their stand upon the Lord's side.*"[37]

Here is something to ponder. The moment will arrive when every individual will have to make a final decision. The things they have read "are influencing their lives," and in the final moments, the publications distributed by missionaries will have exerted their influence. As such, we can only conclude that at a certain time our publications will play the role of *prophets of the eleventh hour.*

Today, our job is to sow—that is, to prepare the ground so that the world stage is set for the moment when God will brighten the world with its last message of mercy. The seeds can then be planted. Then the reaping will be commensurate with the sowing. At that time, many who now appear deaf to the claims of the truth will awaken to embrace it:

"In that day shall the deaf"—that is, those who for various reasons have been prevented from yielding obedience to the truth—"hear the words of the book" (Isa. 29:18). How? The Holy Spirit in latter-rain power will cause the dormant seed to come to life.

While "it is true that some who buy the books will lay them on the shelf or place them on the parlor table," Ellen White assures that "the time will come when these books *will be sought for and read.*"[38] "*God will make many willing to read.*"[39] It is prophecy.

Pastor Alejandro Bullón, when advising us to "sow beside all waters" (Isa. 32:20), observes that "we don't know what result will come from reading a magazine or a book. Its message may seem to have been forgotten. Perhaps a book is left on a dusty shelf, its message ignored and useless. But that book could very well be a time bomb just waiting for its providential moment of impact! Only eternity will reveal the results."[40]

Dire circumstances will soon force people to seriously question everything they now regard as truth. At that juncture, books will provide an answer to millions of people who currently do not attend any church. And though TV and radio can now broadcast truth to millions, we can be sure that under pressing circumstances the government will ban such content. Only those who have a *truth-filled* book or other publication in hand will find refuge from the deadly delusions of the end-time.

Millions attend no church

I want to underscore that many people will never hear the truth unless we take it to them in their homes. And by this I mean taking it and leaving it there *permanently*.

For example, it is commonly stated that the United States, the country that we are told will lead the worldwide movement for Sunday observance, has approximately 100 million people who do not regularly attend any church, and the number is constantly increasing[41] despite the presence of 344,000 houses of worship. How will these millions come to know the truth if we do not bring it to them? How else will they be equipped to make informed decisions?

Speaking of publishing, Ellen White declares: "We cannot too highly estimate this work; for were it not for the efforts of the canvasser, *many would never hear the warning*."[42] She doesn't say that we *should not* estimate it too highly, but, we "*cannot* too highly estimate" it. "By the canvassing work the truth is presented to thousands who otherwise would never hear it."[43]

Will it be different in other countries? Absolutely not.

Sow and multiply much Japanese bamboo

Knowing all this, I invite you, in the name of the Lord, to invest in books that present the gospel of Jesus and His truths for this time. Set apart and consecrate a certain amount of money daily, weekly, or bimonthly so that you are regularly reaching two or three families with the message. Buy books by the caseload and, wherever you are, do not let any opportunity to share them pass you by—and you will be a true evangelist. We must carry forward the work of the sealing.

Are you a student literature evangelist? Remember that God can give you more than just a scholarship if you care about those you visit. Think big. If those who contribute are helping you go back to school, why not help ensure that they get into heaven?

If you do this full-time, renew your strength in the Lord daily so that your efforts to reach families will result in at least one book or magazine being left in every home you visit. Or if you do it on the side, devote more time to it. It is a ministry—a prophetic vocation. And if you are only thinking about literature evangelism, hesitate no more. If the world is to be filled with silent prophets, make it happen!

But there is something greater, something more, that you can do besides distributing or selling the books so necessary for our time. Encourage others to become a part of this sacred ministry. With God's help you can help hasten the return of Jesus.

We are told that we must strive to interest people in books that are of real worth, books that have the Bible as their foundation. But we are also informed that "*it will be a still greater task to find conscientious, God-fearing workers who will enter the field to canvass* for these books for the purpose of diffusing light."[44]

In other words, you must clone. Do not do the work alone. Let's say you are a regular church member who likes to hand out literature—invite others to join you in doing the same. Become a literature distribution leader for your church. Why should you do this? Because "few have broad and extensive views of what can be done in reaching the people by personal, interested efforts in a *wise distribution* of our publications."[45]

Today, given that we still have many church members with a very poor view of the literature ministry, it behooves us to explain its importance. But how? Give them a copy of this book. Simply tell them you would like to know their opinion of what it presents. Since literature evangelism has acquired a poor reputation, we must do everything possible to change the situation. Remember that publishing has a direct relationship to the sealing work. And is anything more important than that?

Bob Hoskins reminds us that "from the point where God first wrote on the tables with His fingers, through the Old Testament and the New Testament to the Reformation, the written Word, the published Word, has been God's method. But the initiative, the drive to print, to publish, to saturate the world with the printed message, has been wrested to a great extent from the church."[46]

If Hoskins' statement is true, how has the church lost its motivation? And is it also true of our beloved Seventh-day Adventist Church?

---

[1] Two places share the name Death Valley: one is in California, U.S.A.; the other is in Atacama, Chile. The documentary focuses on the North American one.

[2] *Los Desiertos* [*The Deserts*], Video Planeta Tierra (México D.F.: BBC, 2006).

[3] See *The Seventh-day Adventist Bible Commentary,* vol. 4, p. 216.

[4] *Ibid.,* p. 225. (Italics supplied.)

[5] E. G. White, *Colporteur Ministry,* p. 151.

[6] Henry Mayhew and Charles Mackay, *The Mormons or Latter-Day Saints* (London: Vizetelly, 1852), p. 276.

[7] See 2 Nephi 27.

[8] http://spanishministries.org/classes/Isaias29.pdf.

[9] Bob Hoskins, *All They Want Is the Truth,* back cover.

[10] *Ibid.,* p. 131.

[11] See http://bookofhope.net.

[12] Hoskins, *All They Want Is the Truth,* p. 130.

[13] Herbert E. Douglass, *Messenger of the Lord* (Nampa, Idaho: Pacific Press Pub. Assn., 1998), p. 362.

[14] Carmelo Martines, "La Metodología de la Misión a Partir de los Textos de la Misión" ["The Methodology of Mission Through the Texts of Mission"], p. 160, http://dialnet.unirioja.es/descarga/articulo/3072092.pdf.

[15] "The canvassing work, properly conducted, is missionary work of the highest order" (E. G. White, *Colporteur Ministry,* p. 6).

[16] See chapters 5 and 6.

[17] Hoskins, *All They Want Is the Truth,* pp. 43, 44. (Italics supplied.)

[18] D. Eastman, *Beyond Imagination,* p. 19.

[19] Ted N. C. Wilson, "Now Is the Time," *Adventist World,* NAD Edition, April 2012, p. 9.

[20] Howard F. Faigao, "Circulating Literature as Never Before," *The Literature Evangelist,* January-March, 2012, p. 3.

[21] Wilmar Hirle, "God's Mail Carriers," *The Literature Evangelist,* July-September 2011, p. 3.

[22] E. G. White, *Colporteur Ministry,* p. 127.

[23] E. G. White, *Christ's Object Lessons,* p. 76.

[24] *Ibid.,* p. 78. (Italics supplied.)

[25] E. G. White, *Colporteur Ministry,* p. 1. (Italics supplied.)

[26] *Ibid.,* p. 6. (Italics supplied.)

[27] In Hoskins, *All They Want Is the Truth,* p. 108.

[28] E. G. White, *Christ's Object Lessons,* p. 79.

[29] E. G. White, *Colporteur Ministry,* p. 150.

[30] E. G. White, *Last Day Events,* p. 212.

[31] E. G. White, *Colporteur Ministry,* p. 128. (Italics supplied.)

[32] E. G. White, *The Great Controversy,* pp. 605, 606. (Italics supplied.)

[33] George R. Knight, *Organizing to Beat the Devil: The Development of Adventist*

Church Structure (Hagerstown, Md.: Review and Herald Pub. Assn., 2001), p. 20. (Italics supplied.)

[34] E. G. White, *Last Day Events,* p. 197. (Italics supplied.)

[35] Rejecting special truths at this time and ignoring the voice of the Holy Spirit at the time of the final conflict may not necessarily be one and the same. Yet we can say for certain that whoever rejects the truth under special circumstances brought on by the Holy Spirit during the final conflict will definitely be severing their connection to God.

[36] *The Seventh-day Adventist Bible Commentary,* Ellen G. White Comments, vol. 6, p. 1055.

[37] E. G. White, *The Great Controversy,* p. 612. (Italics supplied.)

[38] E. G. White, *Colporteur Ministry,* p. 150. (Italics supplied.)

[39] Ellen G. White, *Evangelism* (Washington, D.C.: Review and Herald Pub. Assn., 1946), p. 159. (Italics supplied.)

[40] Alejandro Bullón, *Sharing Jesus Is Everything* (Nampa, Idaho: Pacific Press Pub. Assn., 2010), p. 125.

[41] See George Barna, *Grow Your Church From the Outside In* (Ventura, Calif.: Regal Books, 2002), p. 23.

[42] E. G. White, *Colporteur Ministry,* pp. 6, 7. (Italics supplied.)

[43] *Ibid.,* p. 8.

[44] *Ibid.,* p. 144. (Italics supplied.)

[45] *Ibid.,* p. 8. (Italics supplied.)

[46] Bob Hoskins, *Winning the Race for Russia* (Deerfield, Fla.: Life Publishers Int'l., 1992), pp. 80, 81.

Chapter 5

Prophets That Burn but Are Not Consumed

The police could do nothing about it. The priest had called them, but when they arrived on the scene, the only thing they could say to him was "Sir, for now we still have freedom in this country. Since these men are doing nothing more than exercising their rights, there is nothing we can do against them."

The priest of the Orthodox Church in Austria wanted to stop two Adventists from distributing boxfuls of books not too far from his church.

Aurelian, a literature-distributing member of the Adventist Church, recalls, "This experience motivated [us] to do even more. We don't know how long we will have this freedom. In Romania, thus far, I have never been stopped by an Orthodox priest from distributing these wonderful books—only that once in Austria. So I continue my work, and for the next two months my friend and I will be distributing another 64,000 of them. The year isn't over yet!"[1]

I would not mention Aurelian Anghelescu and his partner Gheorghe Constandis except for the fact that they have already distributed 90,000 books during 10 months in Romania. They are an outstanding example of what church members can do when rightly motivated.

But what was the priest's concern? Why did he try to stop them? The book Aurelian and Gheorghe gave away was *The Great Controversy.*

What worries the mighty of the earth

Literature has power. The premise of this chapter is that we attack what we fear, and the level of energy, time, and effort devoted to destroying that which we fear demonstrates the importance attributed to the object of our dread.

In other words, the magnitude of our attack reveals *what we believe about that which we fear.* If we decide to do away with something, it is because we view it as potential danger.

And who has fought most bitterly against the printed page? Perhaps the most notable thing about the hostility toward it is that it primarily comes from the mighty of the earth. In the words of R. Pattison: "Not every society has chosen to use literacy in the same way, but literacy connected with culture is always power."[2]

Now, why would they want to destroy a book?

Bibliophobia: book fear

Numerous slave owners throughout the nineteenth-century southern United States prohibited their slaves from reading, since their masters feared that they might find revolutionary ideas that could threaten their power.[3]

Maybe the term *bibliophobia* is not the best way to describe the motive by which society has historically waged war against the book. For it was not the books per se that were hated, but the ideas contained in them.

In Nazi Germany, between March and June of 1933 and shortly after Hitler's rise to power, the students, staff, and members of Nazi clubs burned thousands of works written by Marxists, pacifists, and Jewish authors. The great Berlin bonfire of May 10, 1933, consumed works written by such prominent authors as Heinrich Heine, Bertolt Brecht, Franz Kafka, Karl Marx, Heinrich Mann, Kurt Tucholsky, and Carl von Ossietzky, among others. On that one occasion the flames destroyed more than 30,000 books containing ideas hostile to Nazism.[4]

But this is but a minor example of a centuries-long destruction of literary productions. In his volume *Books on Fire*, Lucien X. Polastron emphasizes the never-ending history of the destruction of libraries.[5]

Ray Bradbury's classic, *Fahrenheit 451,* examines this type of censure often imposed by government. The title refers to the temperature at which paper burns. Though the book was written in the mid-1950s, it does an excellent job of describing the background of book burnings. The story depicts a society in which the reading of books is against the law. The inference is that ideas are dangerous, and "thinking outside the box" is discouraged, even outlawed.

Is it better, then, to live in ignorance? To whose benefit might it be for a people to live this way? You will know as we examine a third example of book burning a few pages from now.

Moreover, keep in mind that the power of the book also presupposes a benefit. Juan B. Iguiniz, emphasizing the influence of literature, wrote that "statistics show that the most advanced and cultured peoples, both in intellectual as well as material culture, are those whose bibliographic production is the greatest, that have the most bookstores and, of course, those in which the people read the most."[6]

Still have doubts about the power of the book? Roger Chartier, a specialist in written culture, observes that "the dangerous power of the book is a constant found in Shakespeare's *The Tempest*, where we find a character who must throw his only book overboard, both to rob him of his influence, and second, to break his human will."[7]

Battle for control of the mind

Think about the following: All authors write because they wish to "conquer" other minds. To a great extent an author sets out to influence the world with a given message. It is that simple. Before a single line was written, the mind of the author was *impressed by some idea or thought* that they now want to communicate. Otherwise, what would justify their interest in writing? That which gives significance to writing is the meaning it has to the authors themselves.

In this light the act of writing is a *deliberate* intent to sway the reader. So literature is, in essence, power. That in turn tells us that reading is not something to regard lightly. Writing is a vehicle deliberately used to transfer the authors' thoughts and intents to the reader. We find proof of this in the prefaces, forewords, and introductions of books in which the authors and their associates spell out their deliberate aspirations.

Additional evidence appears in the italics and bold fonts that authors use for emphasis, deliberately leading the readers' minds to certain essential thoughts or ideas.

But here is the reason that governments and religious institutions oppose certain writings: They perceive a very real threat in permanent records of influential ideas. Reading is much more than the conveyance of the spoken word. Radio and television are fundamentally important, but even they do not constitute, as does the book, a lasting physical record readily accessible to the public at any time.

The meaning of book burning

Wikipedia defines book burning as "the practice of destroying, often ceremoniously, books or other written material. In modern times, other forms of media, such as phonograph records, videotapes, and CDs, have also been ceremoniously burned or shredded. Book burning is usually carried out in public, and is generally motivated by moral, religious, or political objections to the material."[8]

We must not, however, view book burning as merely literal. As Roger Chartier points out, "there are many ways to devise book burnings." They could be: "*Repression, Inquisition, auto-da-fé, supression* of everything deemed dangerous to the faith."[9] Each case is tantamount to book burning since all such actions have the same desired effect: *to prevent people from further reading.*

All of this demonstrates that literature has power. More precisely, publishing is not a game. "Words are weapons,"[10] and all the more so when in print. We can find this same hatred of books on the part of governments and institutions in the following incident.

The prophetic book burned before its publication

"Now the king sat in the winterhouse in the ninth month: and there was a fire on the hearth burning before him. And it came to pass, that when Jehudi had read three or four leaves, he cut it with the penknife, and cast it into the fire that was on the hearth, until all the roll was consumed in the fire that was on the hearth" (Jer. 36:22, 23).

According to Scripture, then, what is the aim of burning a book? What does it seek to achieve? As you consider the question, remember that Seventh-day Adventism regards everything that happens in our world as a byproduct of the cosmic conflict between good and evil, between truth and error, between Christ and Satan. Nothing can happen in isolation from those two antagonistic principles and personages.[11]

The burning of the book of Jeremiah was not the result of one man's impulses but of Satan, who hid behind the king's emotions. It was he who moved King Jehoiakim to destroy a portion of Scripture. The message, therefore, made not only the king uncomfortable, *but also the one who stood back of him*: the prince of darkness.

Having answered the question as to why books are burned, we have discovered the principal intent: *to prevent continued reading.* Jehoiakim was nothing more than a puppet of the thoughts and feelings of "spiritual wickedness in high places." "For we wrestle not against flesh and blood, but against principalities, against powers, against the rulers of the darkness of this world" (Eph. 6:12).

However, the destruction of the scroll did not end the matter:

"Take thee again another roll," the Lord commanded His servant, "and write in it all the former words that were in the first roll" (Jer. 36:28). In this way, "the prophet was permitted to reproduce that which the wrath of man would fain have destroyed. . . . The wrath of man had sought to prevent the labors of the prophet of God; but the very means by which Jehoiakim had endeavored to limit the influence of the servant of Jehovah, gave further opportunity for making plain the divine requirements."[12]

"For we can do nothing against the truth, but for the truth" (2 Cor. 13:8).

The real end of the matter was *a new, amplified, and expanded* version of the book of Jeremiah (Jer. 36:32). God would not leave His people without knowledge. Ignorance leads to error and sin:

"My people are destroyed for lack of knowledge," God declared in Hosea 4:6.

Bonfire revived with 50,000 pieces of silver

A second book burning found in the biblical record took place in Ephesus when "many that believed came, and confessed, and shewed their deeds. Many of them also which used curious arts brought their *books together, and burned them* before all men" (Acts 19:18, 19). They were valued at 50,000 pieces of silver.

Here we come to an important point in our study, since reading can be viewed as a danger to the mind when in excess. The idea of derangement as a result of excessive reading is not uncommon. In reality it is just a way of saying that the book has a powerful effect on the individual. The Roman ruler Festus told Paul, "Thou art beside thyself; much learning doth make thee mad" (Acts 26:24). Even wise old Solomon not only suggested but positively stated, in more than one place, that literature has a powerful effect over the individual:

"And further, by these, my son, be admonished: of making many books there is no end; and much study is a weariness of the flesh" (Eccl. 12:12).

Remember that Solomon was a more than average reader and knew what he was talking about.

Looking outside Scripture, we also find other references to the power of literature. If *Quijote de la Mancha* emphasizes nothing else, it is that the book was written with the express purpose of doing away with chivalric romance novels.[13] The main character, Don Quijote, is none other than Alonso Quijano who, according to the novel, loses his mind from reading too many novels. "In short, he became so absorbed in his books that he spent his nights from sunset to sunrise, and his days from dawn to dark, poring over them; and what with little sleep and much reading his brains got so dry that he lost his wits."[14]

Therefore in the burning of occult books, as happened in Ephesus, we see that it took place with the sole purpose of preventing those same books from influencing the minds of the new converts. Had they not destroyed the scrolls, we can only imagine what might have become of that new church.

By this act of book burning the Lord condemned those who practiced magic arts—but at the same time it highlighted the dangers of reading books with the sole purpose of poisoning the mind. This shows that Satan can mastermind the influencing of not only the writers but also the readers of such works.

Given that Satan understands the powerful effect of such literature, he "is busy in this department of his work, scattering literature which is debasing the morals and poisons the minds of the young. Infidel publications are scattered broadcast throughout the land." I believe this is, in part, why Ellen White asks, "Why should not every member of the church be as deeply interested in sending forth publications that will elevate the minds of the people, and bring the truth directly before them? These papers and tracts are for the light of the world, and have often been instrumental in converting souls."[15]

That is why the enemy hates and opposes the publishing program. Such literature is an instrument for salvation, and he knows well the power of the printed page.

The most terrifying book burning the world ever saw

This brings us to the third book burning under study, which took place during the French Revolution. Revelation tells of two witnesses who would prophesy "one thousand two hundred and sixty days, clothed in sackcloth" (Rev. 11:3, NKJV). Those 1,260 days represent 1,260 years, stretching from A.D. 538 through 1798, a period marked by the supremacy of the medieval church. It suppressed the popular study of Scripture—in itself a form of book burning.

Let us ponder this. The two witnesses of the prophecy represent the Old and New Testaments. Jesus stated that the Scriptures testify of Him (John 5:39). And John says that they are the "two candlesticks standing before the God of the earth" (Rev. 11:4). That, of course, is a reference to the Holy Scriptures, which as a candlestick light the way of every person. As David said:

"Thy word is a lamp unto my feet, and a light unto my path" (Ps. 119:105).

In addition, the prophecy emphasizes that the two witnesses have a testimony to give the world. As such, consider this: If a witness is one who speaks in favor of or against something or someone, then the two witnesses who announce the truth as it is in Jesus, and who unmask the deceptions with which the devil tries to entice us, themselves become elements of the war raging between good and evil.

The Bible tells us the beast that "comes up from the Abyss" wages war against the two witnesses, and their bodies then get cast into the city square, where for three and a half days they would be as dead. After that time, the Spirit of life sent from God would enter them and they would stand on their feet. Finally, they would hear a voice from heaven saying, "Come up. . ." placing them forever out of harm's way (Rev. 11:7-12, NIV).

We must not forget that the creation of the Bible societies that sprang up shortly after the French Revolution placed the two witnesses beyond the reach of their enemies, as seen in the proliferation of the Bible around the world.[16] Since this happens at the opening of the time of the end we can better see the reason the enemy of God wages a relentless war against the publishing ministry: *it means the shortening of his life, which is already coming to an end*.

The "three and a half days" refer to the battle that took place in France to replace the religion of the Bible with the deification of human reason. Ellen G. White wrote, "The atheistical power that ruled in France during the Revolution and the Reign of Terror did wage such a war against God and His holy word as the world had never witnessed. . . . Bibles were collected and publicly burned with every possible manifestation of scorn."[17]

All this for the purpose of preventing that beautiful book from further enlightening and transforming the lives of countless thousands. Satan sought to keep people from reading it. Notwithstanding, the Lord knew what was happening to His witnesses. "It was in 1793 that the decrees which abolished the Christian religion and set aside the Bible passed the French Assembly. Three years and a half later a resolution rescinding these decrees, thus granting toleration to the Scriptures, was adopted by the same body."[18]

What is this telling us? If the enemy seeks to prevent the people from reading Scripture, it means that he recognizes an implicit power in it. So how did he learn this?

Real causes of the first deadly wound

Satan has witnessed all the revolutions wrought by books, as well as the abuses perpetrated when humanity lives in abject ignorance. Prior to the deadly wound prophesied against the medieval church's political power (Rev. 13:3), Satan observed the spiritual darkness of the people during the

Middle Ages. And during the French Revolution he attempted a coup de grâce to finish it all. In seeking to eliminate all Bibles, he determined to silence forever the true foundation of all faith. But let us step back a bit. Doesn't the devil know the real causes behind the decline of the Papacy's political power? Doesn't he understand the power of publishing?

Many believe that the deadly wound happened when General Alexandre Berthier deposed Pope Pius VI in 1798. However, that was only the end point of a long, arduous process motivated by *knowledge.* And the press was instrumental in bringing it about.

"What caused this decline in the political power of the Papacy?" Marvin Moore asks. "More than anything else, it was caused by *the revival of learning.*" "As knowledge continued increasing, the papacy's political authority continued declining."[19]

Moore goes on to explain that between the years A.D. 500 and 1000 there came to be a great ignorance about classical Greek and Roman thought. But by the twelfth century the works of ancient thinkers such as Plato and Socrates reappeared. It eventually led to the Renaissance, which started in the fourteenth century and continued through the sixteenth. The arts and literature had a rebirth.

Closely linked to the Renaissance is what we now know as humanism. It emphasizes the importance of the search for rational solutions for humanity's problems instead of blindly accepting those suggested by religion and the church. Knowledge had taken on new strength.

It is also worth noting that the invention or perfectioning of movable type by John Gutenberg in the fifteenth century gave powerful impetus to the availability of knowledge. That produced an intellectual explosion, which resulted in the rapid spread of knowledge.

What did all this accomplish? "People everywhere began thinking for themselves. When people begin to think, they question, and when they question, they start challenging authority."[20]

On top of all this, suddenly the world had the genius of Nicholaus Copernicus (1473-1543), who "discovered" that the earth is not the center of the universe, but that the planets circle the sun. The concept undercut the authority of the church and established the basis for the modern scientific revolution. The revolution of knowledge was triumphing decisively against the ignorance of the times.

But Martin Luther had yet to appear. The Reformation of the sixteenth century was another hard blow on a wound that was not soon to heal. Thanks in large part to the power of the printing press, Luther's "revolutionary" ideas reached the whole European continent in the space of two months. By the time the Vatican could react, it was forever too late.

"Luther's break with Rome would have been impossible without the printing press, which allowed a rapid spread of information. The point is that the increase of knowledge inspired people to challenge authority; in this case, papal authority."[21]

By the eighteenth century the Great Awakening, also known as the Age of Reason, further widened the breach caused by the newly secularized environment. The French Revolution, during which the pope wound up captive in France, came to be seen as the culmination of the revolution of knowledge made possible by the printed page.

Will history repeat itself? The very fact that God has ordained the work of mission-focused literary productions, especially for the time of the end, against a power that will attempt to control the world through heresy and error, suggests that yes, similar events will indeed take place. Babylon will fall once more.

But since the enemy wants to keep people in ignorance we cannot assume that he will sit still:

"Whenever a book is presented that will expose error, Satan is close by the side of the one to whom it is offered, and urges reasons why it should not be accepted. But a divine agency is at work to influence minds in favor of the light."[22]

From Ellen White's statement we can conclude that both God and Satan attribute power to the printed page. Whereas God promotes it, Satan tries to suppress printed truth.

"A great and important work is before us. The enemy of souls realizes this, and he is using every means in his power to lead the canvasser to take up some other line of work. This order of things should be changed. God calls the canvassers back to their work."[23]

Again we note that a relentless war swirls for and against the book. The printed page has tremendous power.

That should give us a sense of why, for the literature evangelist to enjoy success, he or she must pray constantly. They truly are working against principalities that desire to obstruct the circulation of truth. That is why Ellen White warns us:

"Humble, fervent prayer would do more in behalf of the circulation of our books than all the expensive embellishments in the world."[24]

Now the very intensity of the attack, the energy and effort expended to suppress the Bible or any other book containing light, teaches us a valuable lesson: Satan fears greatly the circulation of the truth-filled printed page. The war against the Bible lasted more than a thousand years. For 1,260 years the world witnessed the greatest book burning it has ever known, as religious forces suppressed the Bible or prevented people from reading it. It is a war without end. The enemy knows that the pages containing God's message to the people will have a life-giving effect upon them. But again, how did he learn to fear that power?

What "it is written" means to the devil

In order to answer this question, we must recall that Satan is an excellent student of the words of Scripture. He knows well why God inspired them and their power: "Thy word have I hid in mine heart, that I might not sin against thee" (Ps. 119:11).

The devil understands what the print ministry can do for us, something he learned when he accosted Jesus in the desert. To every temptation he employed to defeat Christ, Jesus met it with an "it is written" (Matt. 4:4, 7, 10).

In fact, knowing the effect of the written word on the mind, the devil himself tried to employ this tactic when he tempted Christ:

"If You are the Son of God, throw Yourself down. For *it is written*: 'He shall give His angels charge over you'" (verse 6, NKJV).

Don't be surprised, then, to find that Satan works continually to thwart the publishing ministry, which threatens to unmask his deceptions. Therefore, when he himself used an "it is written," it tells us he is aware of the power of the printed page to mold peoples' thoughts and actions.

Nadab and Abihu book burnings of today

Given that time is short, what can we expect Satan to try to do to block the true mission of the publishing ministry? His greatest effort will be to "make every effort to magnify in our minds matters of lesser consequence, and to lead us to consider lightly the very work that most needs to be done."[25]

Though at the start of this chapter we mentioned only three book burnings, there is a fourth category more dangerous than all the rest. It is so subtle that we could be repeating the sins of Nadab and Abihu today while we convince ourselves that we are doing God's will. Which book burning am I referring to? The fact that ministers of the printed page, who have been called to be literature evangelists, are selling or giving away books that have little relation to the sealing of the end-time.

Ellen White, in her day, lamented that "there is too much common matter and not enough of the sacred; there is too much dependence upon pictures and other things that do not relate to the vital issues for this time. There is danger of following in the track of Nadab and Abihu, using common in the place of sacred fire."[26]

While it is true that she made the statement to the editors of her time, it continues to have relevance in our day and even speaks to our literature evangelists. The enemy will do all in his power to prevent the publishing ministry from functioning as God designed it. Of equal consequence with book burning is books sitting in storage. What else will the enemy devise? He will work avidly to discourage literature evangelists and to create a poor image of the ministry itself in the churches. And he will succeed if he can cause literature ministry leaders to lose their vision.

Unfortunately, much ignorance fills the church concerning *the importance* of the publishing ministry. Of the 17 million Adventists in the world[27] only about 0.27 percent participate regularly in the distribution of literature. That is close to 46,000 literature evangelists around the world. Think about it—that is *not even 1 percent* of the worldwide church membership. What would happen if the church systematically went about distributing our publications? Fortunately many church members, while not employed as literature evangelists, do avidly share our evangelistic literature as a matter of lifestyle. Michael Ryan, one of our General Conference vice presidents, says, "We should all build a culture of literature distribution." And though many are involved this way, we still find much room for improvement. In chapter 7 we will touch on how each of us can become a messenger of hope.[28]

Saturating our respective countries is realistic

I am inspired by the testimony of Hristo Genchev, who tells that, as a church member in Plovdiv, Bulgaria, "when a new member would come into my church, I always took that person with me to show them how to sell literature. I started educating groups of people on how to work for God. I was driven by a vision of covering the whole region of Plovdiv with books, then reaching all of Bulgaria, then Turkey, and then all of the Muslim world." Later, as the literature director in southern Bulgaria, he came up with "a strategic plan to cover all of Bulgaria with books—*every town, village, and hamlet*."[29] It is just the work that God desires us to do.

And Hristo Genchev is not alone in big dreams. Recently Erton Kohler,

South American Division president, said: "The time has come to witness with power! We must advance in commitment and not lose any opportunity to present the reality of the times we live in and the signs of the soon return of Christ, always emphasizing the coming salvation rather than a coming destruction. We will do so door by door with *The Great Hope*. It is a daring dream, and now is the time! Through the power of the Holy Spirit in every church member, it will become a reality." And he adds: "South America has around 70 million homes, and we want to reach every one between 2012 and 2013. The church has requested 52 million copies for this year, something never before seen in our history. Truly, we are living through a great awakening! Entire cities will be reached in 2012. And we will not stop until we reach 70 million homes, until our message has saturated our entire continent. This is a global movement, throughout the church, and we are going to do our part!"[30]

And what about the United States? Every one of us must play a part in this great missionary undertaking. For example, if 1 million church members each distributed one book a month for the next 10 years, that would equal 120 million homes, the country's entire population.

What if, instead of one book a month, every church member gave away *two* books per month? In less than five years we would have achieved an extraordinary feat. It represents a monthly investment of approximately $4.00. Clearly we need to lay out bigger, more aggressive plans.

I wonder what eternity will hold for each church member who decides to contact his or her neighborhood, town, or a whole city. Ellen White offers encouragement:

"Think of how great a work can be done if a large number of believers will unite in an effort to place before the people, by the circulation of these books, the light that the Lord has said should be given them. Under divine guidance, go forward in the work, and look to the Lord for aid. The Holy Spirit will attend you. Angels of heaven will accompany you, preparing the way."[31]

I pray that we take up the work that is beginning in many places, that every passing week we can see more and more committed members distributing, in a systematic, orderly fashion, books to both rich and poor. I pray that chosen literature evangelists would visit the elite of society as well as saturate office buildings everywhere with our books and periodicals. I pray that we shall soon see literature ministry leaders with a strong, clear vision of what our publications can do for the world, and will give it a decided push.

Is it possible? Would many more be saved?

[1] Gabriel Maurer, "For the Moment We Have Freedom," *The Literature Evangelist*, January-March 2009, p. 12.

[2] Robert Pattison, *On Literacy: The Politics of the Word From Homer to the Age of Rock* (New York: Oxford, 1982), p. viii.

[3] http://en.wikipedia.org/wiki/Education_during_the_Slave_Period.

[4] "Libros Quemados por las Nazis" ["Nazi Book Burning"], www.cpdhcorrientes.com.ar/libroquemado.htm.

[5] Lucien X. Polastron, *Libros En Llamas: Historia De la Interminable Destrucción De Bibliotecas* [*Books on Fire: The Destruction of Libraries Throughout History*], (México D.F.: Fondo De Cultura Económica, 2007), pp. 297-301.

[6] Juan B. Iguiniz, *El Libro, Epítome de Bibliología* [*The Book, Epítome of Bibliology*] (México D.F.: Editorial Porrúa, 1998), p. 213.

[7] In Alberto Cue, *Cultura Escrita, Literatura e Historia* [*Written Culture, Literature and History: Conversations With Roger Chartier*] (México D.F.: Fondo de Cultura Económica, 1999), p. 158.

[8] http://en.wikipedia.org/wiki/Book_burning.

[9] Cue, p. 33.

[10] Robert B. Downs, *Books That Changed the World* (New York: Signet Classic, 2004), p. 1.

[11] E. G. White, *Education,* pp. 169, 170, 185.

[12] Ellen G. White, *Prophets and Kings* (Mountain View, Calif.: Pacific Press Pub. Assn., 1917), p. 437.

[13] Miguel de Cervantes Saavedra, *Don Quijote de la Mancha* (México D.F.: Editorial Época, S.A., 2006), p. 13.

[14] Miguel de Cervantes, *The History of Don Quixote de la Mancha*, trans. John Ormsby, Great Books of the Western World (Chicago: Encyclopaedia Britannica, 1952), vol. 29, pp. 1, 2.

[15] E. G. White, *Christian Service*, p. 146.

[16] L. Wade, *El Futuro del Mundo Revelado en el Apocalipsis,* pp. 146, 147.

[17] E. G. White, *The Great Controversy*, p. 273.

[18] *Ibid.*, p. 287.

[19] M. Moore, *Could It Really Happen?* pp. 47, 49.

[20] *Ibid.*, p. 48.

[21] *Ibid.*, p. 49.

[22] E. G. White, *Colporteur Ministry,* p. 115.

[23] *Ibid.*, p. 13.

[24] *Ibid.*, p. 80.

[25] *Ibid.*, p. 38.

[26] E. G. White, *Counsels to Writers and Editors,* pp. 112, 113.

[27] By the most recent report at the time of writing: http://docs.adventistarchives.org//docs/stats/2ndQtrSecReportWorldSum2011.pdf.

[28] http://greatcontroversyproject.adventist.org/assets/files/GCP12.08.11.pdf.

[29] Hristo Genchev, "An Arrow in God's Hand," *The Literature Evangelist*, April-September 2007, pp. 14, 15.

[30] See http://www.portaladventista.org.

[31] E. G. White, *Colporteur Ministry,* p. 22.

Chapter 6

Prophets That Save Multitudes

If indeed our church is not to be wholly dependent on mass media outlets in order to further its message on a large scale, a nagging question faces us as we near what we expect to be a prohibitive political environment: If the printed page is to carry on the work of our mass media outlets once the latter are banned from the airwaves, what should be our strategy in our current literature ministry? Who will accept truth and be finally saved? What does this have to do with a great multitude? We will explore these questions in this chapter.

Alejandro Bullón says, "It's a thrill every time people . . . say that they came to know the gospel as a result of a book or an article I [wrote]. I know that someday, walking down the golden street of the new earth, I will meet many people who . . . never heard me preach, but who [have] read one of the books I have written."[1]

How can the printed page have such power? Could a single written work bring earth within heaven's reach? I feel that it can.

A parable "from beneath" on methods of evangelism

In Luke 16 we find an interesting dialogue between "Abraham" and a rich man. At first glance it appears to be a parable about hell, but the language Jesus employs is not literal in the least. For example, it is absurd to think that the tip of a finger dipped in water would be enough to soothe the rich man burning in hell. Agreed? Then what is the parable really about?

Scholars explain that it contains three very clear arguments. Among them: "The Scriptures are a sufficient witness to lead us to repent and to follow [biblical ethics]."[2] By implication, the same must necessarily be true of the printed page that bears the message of the Bible.

Ellen White confirms this by explaining that the parable teaches us that "the law and the prophets are God's appointed agencies for the salvation of men," and adds, "Those who heed Moses and the prophets will require no greater light than God has given." She also emphasizes, "If man fails to do that which a little light shows to be his duty, greater light would only reveal unfaithfulness, neglect to improve the blessings given."[3]

Furthermore, she tells us that the lesson we must draw from the parable is "that *every man is given sufficient light* for the discharge of the duties required of him."[4] And she supports her statement with Scripture:

"He that is faithful in that which is least is faithful also in much: and he that is unjust in the least is unjust also in much" (Luke 16:10).

The passage appears in the context of a person who complains to God about not having been adequately warned. The Lord denies his request by refusing to allow Lazarus to tend to his needs. His probation has ended. But now the man's petition changes. Pretending missionary zeal, he asks that Lazarus be sent in person to witness to his five living brothers, "lest *they also* come into this place of torment" (verse 28).

Here we see the rich man's good intentions in wanting to see his brothers saved, but he asks for the method that *he* thinks is the best: a living person present to provide a spoken witness. However, "Abraham" responds in the negative, telling him that "they have Moses and the prophets" (verse 29) as sufficient evidence for salvation.

In other words, God is telling the rich man that a living, spoken testimony will not improve matters. The man rejects or dislikes the idea of entrusting the printed page with his living brothers' salvation. He refuses to believe such a condition is enough. And so he retorts, "Nay, father Abraham: But if one went unto them from the dead, they will repent" (verse 30).

What the rich man is really saying is "That is not enough! That approach is not sufficient to provide my brothers a saving witness. Only the printed page? No way!"

A human being pretended to know better than God. At the same time he was really implying that if God had warned him sufficiently, he would not be in that place. But that is nothing other than putting the blame on God for the loss of his own soul. The Lord ignores his claim and reiterates His answer with firmness: "If they hear not Moses and the prophets, neither will they be persuaded, though one rose from the dead" (verse 31).

Jesus' parable confirms what He said on another occasion:

"For had ye believed Moses, ye would have believed me: for he *wrote* of me. But *if ye believe not his writings, how shall ye believe my words?*" (John 5:46, 47).

Tragically, the lesson was not learned, and Jesus' words were fulfilled to the very letter, being confirmed in the resurrection of Lazarus. Even after seeing Lazarus resurrected, the religious leaders refused to believe in Jesus.

Therefore, by implication we can safely conclude that seemingly nothing stands above the written word. The Lord will see His purposes accomplished through it, since the purpose for which He established it is clear: The written Word contains the seal of God's approval, is His witness, and according to the message of the parable, those who refuse to believe what God has said in it will not believe in any other way.

Is the written testimony biblical?

Jesus said, "Search the scriptures; for in them ye think ye have eternal life: and they are they which testify of me" (John 5:39). Here He confirms that the role of "Scripture" is to witness. In effect He is saying that if witnessing means to speak for or against something or someone, the written word has been authorized to do so. A written witness! And it is true of any writing, not only Scripture. All writing has this function. Consider Peter's words: "I have written briefly, exhorting, and *testifying* that this is the true grace of God wherein ye stand" (1 Peter 5:12).

Put another way, the apostle is simply saying that he is witnessing through the act of writing his letter. His letter declares that "this is the true grace of God wherein ye stand." The writings themselves communicate grace.

So yes, the Bible teaches that written documents witness, preach, and proclaim the truth. And isn't that what God desires? The author of Hebrews also confirms this:

"But one *in a certain place testified*, saying, What is man, that thou art mindful of him? or the son of man, that thou visitest him?" (Heb. 2:6).

The one witnessing was King David. The "certain place" refers to Psalm 8:4, the passage cited. And the "testified" indicates what David was doing through his writing. *He was witnessing through the words he would write.*

We then see that to witness includes more than just speaking or living what is right. Writing, too, is a method of witnessing. And taking the books to the homes of the people is to provide that very testimony the world most needs. It is in this sense that the Old and New Testaments are the "two witnesses" that will "prophesy" and give "their testimony" to the whole world (Rev. 11:2, 7). Moreover, that same written witness will leave the world without an excuse. And the fact that it does so is proof in itself that it has power to save them.

Jack Goody observes that "in the sphere of religion, *it is significant that the religions of conversion*, the excluding religions, *are all religions of the book.*" Later he adds, "All the 'world religions' are literate religions."[5] That is, they all make use of the written word to extend their doctrines. In negative terms, it means that not using the printed page is the worst policy any religion can adopt. Those that understand its power employ it on a large scale.

Goody himself comments that "considering the importance of writing over the past 5,000 years, and the *profound effects* it has on the lives of each and all, surprisingly little attention has been given to the way in which it has influenced the social life of mankind."[6]

What might those effects be if they can be found in Scripture?

Biblical foundations and writing for salvation

Paul wrote, "For though I made you sorry *with a letter*, I do not repent, though I did repent: for I perceive that *the same epistle* hath made you sorry, though it were but for a season.

Now I rejoice, not that ye were made sorry, but that ye sorrowed to repentance: for ye were made sorry after a godly manner" (2 Cor. 7:8, 9).

Notice that the apostle, as is surely true of many writers since, was not completely sure what the effect of that message might be. Paul used the expression "though I did repent" to indicate that he couldn't be certain of the ultimate results. But he realized afterward that God, who motivated him to write, had a salvational purpose to fulfill through that "written page." It led to a heartfelt repentance among the Corinthians.

Here we see that Paul, by divine inspiration, attributed that repentance to a written letter. And as surely as we cannot credit that epistle as being the *sole* agent behind that transformation, it is just as certain that the Holy Spirit availed Himself of that letter (the written word) in helping to bring about a much-needed experience.

Indeed, it is most revealing that Paul used the expression "after a godly manner" (sort) three times in referring to that exchange (verses 9-11). First he stated his letter made them sad, but then observed that it was "a godly" sorrow, one according to God's will—he intended it to be so. Notice that the apostle claimed that God wanted for that writing to lead to that experience. As a result, he ends by declaring, "Wherefore, though I wrote unto you, I did it not for his cause that had done the wrong, nor for his cause that suffered wrong, but that our care for you in the sight of God might appear unto you" (verse 12).

Now let's look at the case of the Berean church members:

"These were more noble than those in Thessalonica, in that they received the word with all readiness of mind, and searched the scriptures daily, *whether those things were so*" (Acts 17:11).

The verse reveals that the Bereans did not believe based solely on Paul's preaching, but rather because they also searched the Word of God to confirm whether what the apostle told them was true or not:

"Therefore many of them believed; also of honourable women which were Greeks, and of men, not a few" (verse 12).

Scripture emphasizes the fact that once the Bereans examined the truth of Paul's words by consulting the written record, *they believed—not because someone preached to them, but because of the written testimony. The Twentieth Century New Testament* renders the verse this way:

"*As a consequence*, many of them became believers in Christ."[7]

We find, then, further confirmation of the role played by the printed page in the conversion of the Bereans.

I want to note that the expression "Therefore, many of them believed" is not the same as saying "So many of them believed." This last phrasing would weaken the power of what the Holy Spirit is really trying to tell us—that the Bereans were converted through methods devised by the Holy Spirit. The Bible points out the key role of the written testimony in that wonderful conversion.

The original Greek reads *men oun,* commonly translated as "therefore, in this way." The article character *men* denotes contrast, emphasis, or continuity, and when accompanied by *oun* is generally translated as "therefore, in this way."[8]

In sum, the fact that many believed indicates the faith of the Bereans, and the "therefore" tells us that it happened in part through the written proclamation of the truth.

We see the same result in Acts 16, in which Paul and Silas traveled about confirming the churches:

"And as they went through the cities, they delivered them the decrees for to keep, that were ordained of the apostles and elders which were at Jerusalem" (Acts 16:4).

Bear in mind that the apostles and elders commissioned Paul and Silas to deliver to the churches the written agreement voted on the controversy about circumcision (Acts 15:1-5).

"So when they were dismissed, they came to Antioch; and when they had gathered the multitude together, they delivered the epistle, which, when they had read, they rejoiced for the consolation" (verses 30, 31).

Acts 16 tells us that Paul, as he went through the cities, presented the agreements decided by the apostles and elders at Jerusalem (verse 4). And what was the result? Scripture announces:

"And so were the churches established in the faith, and increased in number daily" (verse 5).

Just as with the Bereans, we notice here that the confirmation of the faith of the believers and the increase in the membership resulted once again from the written ministry. The King James Version translates *men oun* with the words "and so." It makes clear that the dogmata (ordinances), writings that Paul delviered to the churches, played a vital role in the salvation of the faithful. The word "so" is the same as saying "in this way." In other words, this is the way the writings participated in the spread and preaching of the gospel in the time of the apostles.

Seven biblical reasons to use the printed page

How valuable is the printed page in evangelism? Highly. And it is so primarily because God has so desired it. And what is His intent? Paul declared that God is interested "for all men; for kings, and for all that are in authority" (1 Tim. 2:1, 2) and adds, "Who will have all men to be saved, and to come unto the knowledge of the truth" (verse 4).

We see here not one, but two desires: that all human beings might be saved and that they might come to a knowledge of the truth. But is it biblical to believe that the Scriptures amply fulfill the twin purposes? Absolutely. Let's examine those seven great reasons.

1. Literature awakens understanding and leads to investigation

Peter wrote, "This second epistle, beloved, I now write unto you; *in both which* I stir up your pure minds by way of remembrance: *that ye may be mindful* of the words which were spoken before by the holy prophets" (2 Peter 3:1, 2).

It is another way of saying that literature can perform the role of sentinels whose mission is to awaken the people and alert them to imminent danger. Such is our task. God charges us with warning the wicked so that they may save themselves and we be cleared of their blood. Is this not God's charge to His prophets? Our publications fulfill the same purpose.

We are clear, then, that the spoken message is insufficient:

"Though the minister may faithfully present the message, the people are not able to retain it all. The printed page is therefore essential, not only in awakening them to the importance of the truth for this time, but in rooting and grounding them in the truth and establishing them against deceptive error."[9]

2. The mission of publishing: to warn an entire world

Continuing the above trend of thought, let us contemplate what the apostle Peter wrote:

"I have written briefly, *exhorting*, and testifying that this is the true grace of God wherein ye stand" (1 Peter 5:12).

Since the passage appears in one of the "general" epistles, it underscores the wide application of the exhortation.

In the same way, Paul states that the reason we have a written record of the things that overtook Israel in the desert is that "all these things happened unto them for ensamples: and they are written for our admonition, upon whom the ends of the world are come" (1 Cor. 10:11).

The word "admonition" renders the Greek term *noutesian*, which we can translate as "teaching, warning, or exhortation." If the biblical authors composed their writings with that express purpose, then what we distribute to the world in our days helps us to fulfill our very specific mission, as delineated in Revelation 14.

Ellen White can say with all confidence, "All who consecrate themselves to God to work as canvassers are assisting to give the last message of *warning* to the world."[10]

3. Literature molds people's minds

Paul wrote: "That ye be not soon shaken in mind, or be troubled, neither by spirit, nor by word, nor by letter as from us, as that the day of Christ is at hand" (2 Thess. 2:2).

Speaking to us through the apostle, the Holy Spirit attributes power to the written word to mold the human mind:

"This agency can reach and influence the public mind *as no other means can*."[11] And we are reassured that the "silent messengers are enlightening and molding the minds of thousands [of persons] in every country and in every clime."[12]

Isn't it amazing that despite such glowing assurances of this ministry's place, many are happy doing next to nothing?

4. Literature teaches and indoctrinates

The book of Romans says that the "things that were written before were written for our learning, that we through the patience and comfort of the Scriptures might have hope" (Rom. 15:4, NKJV). The word "learning" comes from the Greek *didaskalias*, and can be translated as "teaching" or "doctrine." It is the same word that Paul used later on in his writing (2 Tim. 3:10, 16). For example, when he declares that the scriptures are "profitable for teaching," he employs the word. On the other hand, it is the same vocabulary that he uses to tell Timothy that he, Timothy, has understood "the doctrine" of the apostle, something Jannes and Jambres did not.

The written page's role of teaching and indoctrinating is in accordance with the great commission of Jesus, the Word. We read:

"Go ye therefore, and teach all nations, baptizing them in the name of the Father, and of the Son, and of the Holy Ghost: teaching them to observe all things whatsoever I have commanded you" (Matt. 28:19, 20).

Ellen White reminds us:

"Our publications have a most sacred work to do in making clear, simple, and plain the spiritual basis of our faith."[13] She adds that the church "should be impressed with the importance of bringing before the world as fast as possible the books necessary for their spiritual education and enlightenment."[14]

Put another way, they must teach and indoctrinate the world. What other reason could there be for writing and publishing them? As Paul said: "Therefore, brethren, stand fast, *and hold the traditions which ye have been taught*, whether by word, *or our epistle*" (2 Thess. 2:15).

We see once again in this verse textual evidence that the believers in Thessalonica learned doctrine, in part, through the evangelistic ministry of the printed page—the written preacher. Would the Holy Spirit work through us as He did through Paul and the other apostles, using our own written material? Think of it: We ourselves have been indoctrinated in the truth via the printed page and, in some cases, actual letters of people who cared enough to write to us.

5. Literature leads people to understand truth better

To more clearly grasp this point, let us examine the book of Luke. Here we see what motivated the document bearing his name. The word "that" sometimes identifies the reason a person undertakes an action, and Luke tells Theophilus, "That *you may know the certainty* of those things in which you have been instructed" (Luke 1:4, NKJV).

The language employed also indicates that Theophilus is someone who already to some degree has been instructed into a body of knowledge, but who nonetheless lacks a full and complete account. In this case he represents the millions of people among us who lack a complete and systematic account of the things preached in our day.

And by distributing our publications many of us have been doing the work once done by the wise Solomon when he said, "Have I not written to thee excellent things in counsels and knowledge, that I might *make thee know the certainty of the words of truth*; that thou might answer the words of truth to them that send unto thee?" (Prov. 22:20, 21).

All this teaches us that inspired writing is an essential ministry with its own role in fulfilling God's desire for the world.

"The Lord has sent His message to the world *in books that contain the truth for the last days*."[15] And Ellen White reminds us that the "great object of our publications is to exalt God, *to call men's attention to the living truths of His word*."[16]

6. Literature saves

Anyone who doubts the role of literature in converting people should consider the following passage:

"And many other signs truly did Jesus in the presence of his disciples, which are not written in this book: But *these are written, that ye might believe* that Jesus is the Christ, the Son of God; *and that believing ye might have life* through his name" (John 20:30, 31).

The reason the biblical authors recorded the actions of Jesus among His disciples is so that we might believe on Him and, as a result, be saved.

The work of reaching people through the printed page is not merely a human invention. John was compelled to record why he resorted to the book. Sanctified writings are an essential vehicle of salvation. Paul understood this well when he wrote to Timothy:

"And that from a child thou hast known the holy scriptures, which are able to make thee wise unto salvation through faith which is in Christ Jesus" (2 Tim. 3:15).

Therefore books containing truth that leads to Christ have great potential to save human beings.

It should come as no surprise, then, to find Ellen White pleading, "The canvassing work is a most successful way of saving souls. Will you not try it?"[17]

How successful? As a result it will lead many into the truth:

"Our publications are now sowing the gospel seed, and *are instrumental in bringing as many souls to Christ as the preached word*. Whole churches have been raised up as the result of their circulation."[18]

7. Literature settles and confirms believers in truth

Once peoples have given themselves to Christ, is there anything more literature can do for them? Assuredly. Literature settles people into truth:

"I have not written unto you because ye know not the truth, but because ye know it, and that no lie is of the truth" (1 John 2:21).

Here we find a written record establishing new believers into truth. Paul described similar circumstances:

"To write the same things to you, to me indeed is not grievous, but for you it is safe" (Phil. 3:1).

He too is grounding his new converts in truth.

It is difficult to overemphasize its importance. The wave of deception and false doctrine sweeping the world calls for a decided work of settling minds into the oracles of God, for Satan will stop at nothing in his aim of bringing the whole world, including the elect, to complete perdition. Literature is indispensable.

"In enlightening and confirming souls in the truth, the publications will *do a far greater work* than can be accomplished by the ministry of the word alone."[19]

This "far greater work" will intensify at the commencement of the final crisis, when it will fill in for the absence of literature evangelists and TV, radio, and Internet evangelism.

8. Prophets that save multitudes

Thus far, all the points we have covered are biblical reasons it is crucial that we take up literature evangelism. Yet we need to consider something even more fundamental: Do you understand why *you* should be doing this?

If the printed page is to stand in for our mass media outlets in the final crisis, how many can the method actually reach? Which is to ask, How important is it? We know that *"more than one thousand* will soon be converted in one day, most of whom will trace their first convictions to the reading of our publications."[20] But there is something deeper here.

In the third chapter we established that the church participates in the sealing work with a writer's case or writer's inkhorn, using the written word to accomplish its mission. So the question arises: Is there a link between the sealing of the 144,000 *and* the great uncounted multitude of Revelation 7:9? Beatrice S. Neall observes that "although Adventists have [traditionally] separated the 144,000 from the great multitude seen before the throne in the interlude's closing scene, evidence supports the belief that they are one and the same group. That is, the sealed 144,000 *symbolize* the great multitude from every nation, kindred, and tongue who will remain loyal to God in the closing conflict of the great controversy between God and Satan."[21]

Most recently, Ekkehardt Mueller wrote that "the 144,000 and the great multitude are one and the same." That is, "they are the same group under different names."[22] Which leads to the conclusion that through the evangelistic mass media venues now at its disposal, and by its relation to the sealing work, literature evangelism results in the salvation not just of a literal 144,000 but of a great multitude, something doubly motivating to our outreach efforts.

Now, given that the 144,000 and the great multitude *are one and the same*,[23] logically the great multitude is also sealed,[24] and our efforts should aim to reach this massive body. Therefore, our printing houses should, in relation to the funding allotted them, produce all the literature they can—*by the millions*—and the entire church must participate in the mass distribution if we are to see the sealing work among the great multitude.

"God calls for workers from every church among us to enter His service as canvasser evangelists," Ellen White wrote. "Through its faithful ministrations, *a multitude that no man can number* will become children of God, fitted for the everlasting glory."[25]

Our responsibility is not simply to convert people, but to accomplish the *sealing of multitudes*. Shall we stand back now? No. LaRondelle suggests that Revelation 11:13 indicates that those who repent are not a minority but a majority.[26]

Jon Paulien wrote: "Revelation 11:13 makes it clear that many of those in Babylon will respond favorably. This final 'remnant' could even become a majority, at least in some segments of Babylon."[27]

So what should be our goal? To reach a local territory or the whole world? Our mission is to that great multitude. And since it is the church's responsibility to spearhead the dissemination of the sealing message, what are the best methods to go about it?

---

[1] A. Bullón, *Sharing Jesus Is Everything*, p. 124.

[2] Tom Shepherd, "Interpretation of Biblical Types, Allegories, and Parables," in George W. Reid, ed., *Understanding Scripture: An Adventist Approach*, Biblical Research Institute Studies (Silver Spring, Md.: Biblical Research Institute, 2005), vol. 1, p. 240.

[3] E. G. White, *Christ's Object Lessons*, p. 265.

[4] *Ibid.* (Italics supplied.)

[5] Jack Goody, *Literacy in Traditional Societies* (Cambridge, U.K.: Cambridge Univ. Press, 2005), pp. 2, 9. (Italics supplied.)

[6] *Ibid.*, p. 1. (Italics supplied.)

[7] *The New Testament From 26 Translations* (Grand Rapids: Zondervan, 1967), p. 548.

[8] *The Greek New Testament* (New York: United Bible Societies, 1975), pp. 115, 127.

[9] E. G. White, *Colporteur Ministry*, p. 100.

[10] *Ibid.*, p. 6. (Italics supplied.)

[11] *Ibid.*, p. 149. (Italics supplied.)

[12] *Ibid.*, p. 5.

[13] *Ibid.*, p. 1.

[14] *Ibid.*, p. 6.

[15] *Ibid.*, p. 138. (Italics supplied.)

[16] *Ibid.*, p. 2. (Italics supplied.)

[17] *Ibid.*, p. 37.

[18] *Ibid.*, p. 150. (Italics supplied.)

[19] *Ibid.,* p. 100. (Italics supplied.)

[20] *Ibid.,* p. 151. (Italics supplied.)

[21] Beatrice S. Neall, "Sealed Saints and the Tribulation," *Symposium on Revelation,* book 1, p. 245. See also H. K. LaRondelle, *How to Understand the End-Time Prophecies of the Bible,* pp. 153-156.

[22] Ekkehardt Mueller, "Who Are the 144,000 and the Great Multitude?" *Interpreting Scripture,* ed. Gerhard Pfandl (Silver Spring, Md.: Biblical Research Institute, 2010), vol. 2, pp. 433, 434.

[23] Hans LaRondelle points out that "it is important to note that John does *not* state that he *saw* 144,000 Israelites as the sealed. He states only that he '*heard the number*' (Rev. 7:4). When John turned to see the sealed ones, he saw only a great multitude of conquerors. This word-picture confirms the gospel truth that the promises of God to Israel will not fail but will be fulfilled in Christ and His people. The pattern of *hearing* and then turning to *see* was used by John in Revelation 1:12, 13. What John heard is then further clarified by what he actually sees. Another instance is found in Revelation 5. He hears an elder declare: 'See, the Lion of the tribe of Judah . . . has triumphed" (Rev. 5:5). But when he looks to see the Lion, he 'saw a Lamb, looking as if it had been slain, standing in the center of the throne' (Rev. 5:6). What John *saw* was a clarification of what he had first only *heard.* This style of disclosure is used also by John in Revelation 7. After he had *heard* the number of Israelites who were sealed, John '*looked* and there before me was a great multitude that no one could count, from every nation, tribe, people and language, standing before the throne and in front of the Lamb' (Rev. 7:9). In a later vision John sees the 144,000 also 'before the throne' (Rev. 14:3) while they 'follow the Lamb wherever he goes' (Rev. 14:4). Thus John identifies the 144,000 spiritual Israelites as the countless believers in Christ, the Lamb of God. . . . The true Israel of God is not limited to 144,000 literal Jews, but is symbolic of the totality of spiritual Israel among the human race" (*How to Understand the End-Time Prophecies of the Bible,* p. 149).

[24] Marvin Moore adds that even "those who believe the 144,000 and the great multitude are two groups also believe that the great multitude will be sealed before the close of probation, just [as] the 144,000, even though Revelation 7:9-17 does not mention that. They would have to be sealed in order to live without a Mediator after the close of probation" (*The Crisis of the End-Time* [Nampa, Idaho: Pacific Press Pub. Assn., 1992], p. 142).

[25] E. G. White, *Colporteur Ministry,* p. 20. (Italics supplied.)

[26] See LaRondelle, pp. 230, 231.

[27] J. Paulien, *Armageddon at the Door,* pp. 170, 171.

Chapter 7

Prophets Proclaiming All Around You

Dear reader, do not read this chapter unless you have decided whole-heartedly to place yourself fully in God's hands to help prepare the ground for the latter-rain power before Jesus comes. Unless you wish to make a real difference in the proclamation of the gospel, stop now. Or do you wish to continue?

Consider this: Can something be done so that the whole church gets involved in the preaching of the gospel? If we can't pull it off, God will have no other recourse but to employ different people using a plan unknown to us. But God's desire is to have everyone participate. It is in this vein that Ellen White wrote: "The great outpouring of the Spirit of God, which lightens the whole earth with His glory, *will not come until we have an enlightened people, that know by experience what it means to be laborers together with God.*"[1]

How will the church meet such a requirement?

George Verwer points out that the "population explosion . . . has caused Christian leaders to conclude that if the entire world is ever to hear of Christ, the church must become totally involved in world evangelism.

"There is a general agreement that one of the key ingredients in the fulfilling of this great responsibility is the increased use of literature."

Many believe that the only way to reach all people with the gospel *is through the printed page.*[2]

Dale E. Galusha, president of Pacific Press Publishing Association, observes that "no other means of reaching out for souls can ever take the place of literature."[3] Is such a view too simplistic in its approach? Absolutely not.

Ellen White wrote that "when we follow plans of the Lord's devising, we are 'laborers together with God.' Whatever our position—whether presidents of conferences, ministers, teachers, students, or lay members—we are held accountable by the Lord for making the most of our opportunities to enlighten those in need of present truth. And *one of the principal agencies He has ordained* for our use is the printed page."[4]

Author Dick Eastman has pointed out that "God's plans are always incredibly simple and unusually inexpensive. So if things start getting terribly complex and amazingly expensive, you might rethink whether it's God's plan after all."[5] And since the Seventh-day Adventist Church has had an active philosophy of literature distribution, have we been executing it properly?

George R. Knight reminds us that "major restructuring in Adventism's past *has consistently revolved around being more efficiently equipped for mission.*" And he adds, "If Adventism is to be consistent with its past, any future reorganization will have to focus on more effectively coordinating worldwide mission in such a way that it spends less money on support structures, thus freeing up more funds . . . for 'frontline' endeavors."[6]

If there is one approach that also happens to be extremely economical, it is that of literature distribution. As Gabriel Zaid has said of books: "No cheaper means to address so few people—so widely dispersed in place and time—has ever been invented."[7] And when mass-circulated, *it becomes incredibly economical.* Other methods can be extremely expensive and slow, and nothing remains behind with the people to proclaim the message.

Now listen to what Paul has to say:

"Now to him that is of power to stablish you according to my gospel, and the preaching of Jesus Christ, according to the revelation of the mystery, which was kept secret since the world began, but now is made manifest, and by the scriptures of the prophets, according to the commandment of the everlasting God, made known to all nations for the obedience of faith" (Rom. 16:25, 26).

According to the apostle, God has a plan for the world and for the books written by the prophets. In accordance with God's will, through this medium the world will yield obedience to the faith. Another translation expresses the thought this way:

"We now know this plan *through what was written by the prophets.* Moreover, the Eternal God *commanded it this way,* so that the whole world will believe and obey the Lord."[8]

Can it be any clearer? Paul is suggesting a worldwide evangelization through literature. The people of the Bible were firm believers in the missionary power of Scripture. For example, did you know that Ezra was a literature evangelist? Five hundred years before Christ we find a believer in the power of the printed page:

"During the captivity the knowledge of God's will had to some extent been lost. *Ezra gathered all the copies of the law that he could find.* He published copies of these among God's people, and became a teacher of the law and the prophecies in the schools of the prophets. The pure Word, thus diligently taught by Ezra, gave knowledge that was invaluable at that time."[9]

Ezra was truly a minister of the printed page who, though he did not sell his literature, communicated God's message in written form.

"For Ezra had prepared his heart to seek the law of the Lord, and to do it, and to teach in Israel statutes and judgments" (Ezra 7:10).

Willing to do God's will where he was placed, he sought support in the written ministry to carry out God's purposes. As such, Ezra was a perfect example of what every church member must be in our time.

Scant progress happens without the printed page

In 1874, after a series of presentations made in Rome, New York, by several ministers, Ellen White received a dream. She saw a youth of noble bearing who entered her room immediately after she spoke. He told her that "unless there is a more thorough effort made to fasten these impressions upon minds, your efforts will prove nearly fruitless. Satan has many attractions ready to divert the mind. . . . In every effort such as you are now making, much more good would result from your labors if you had appropriate reading matter ready for circulation."[10]

On another occasion she stated that Adventists were "not doing *one twentieth part* of the work we should for the salvation of souls."[11] Not much later her accompanying angel declared, "You are not as a people doing *one twentieth* part of what might be done in spreading the knowledge of the truth. *Very much more can be accomplished* by the living preacher with the circulation of papers and tracts *than by the preaching of the word alone without the publications.* The press is a powerful instrumentality which God has ordained *to be combined* with the energies of the living preacher to bring the truth before all nations, kindreds, tongues, and peoples. Many minds can be reached *in no other way.*"[12]

What is significant about this last quote is that it is an assessment made by a heavenly visitor about what Adventists were conducting back then. And in effect he is telling us that unless we combine publications with the living preacher, we are doing a half-baked job. Some would protest that we have finally started following this advice. While true, many others see even our latest efforts as extremely mild.

Jehovah's Witnesses believe in literature so strongly that they distribute approximately 88 million copies of their magazines every month. It adds up to more than 1 billion copies per year.[13]

Now if they, who lack the breadth of the knowledge of truth that we enjoy, can put such far-reaching, well-organized plans for literature into operation, shouldn't we be expected to exert even greater effort, given our understanding that we have the last warning message to the world?

In the end, *publications are as the wings of the message.* Speed and swiftness in the circulation of the message has more to do with the printed page than with the living preacher. And when we combine the two, as we are discussing here, then things really take off.

Why is it better to combine the two ways of delivering the message? Because we find their greater effectiveness represented in the bread multiplied by Christ's hands (Mark 6:35-44). Ellen White specifically tells that "thus it will be in the distribution of our publications," and that the truth, "as it is passed out, will multiply greatly."[14] Without a doubt, a single book can provide spiritual food for many.

Now, given that the gospel has been introduced in many countries, including our own, through the activity of the literature evangelist and the printed page, wouldn't it be well to print thousands and commission literary workers to preach everywhere, to all classes, and in many languages? The problem is that as an organization we have a culture of evangelism focused on the living preacher, and the local church generally has not participated in a systematic use of the printed page. Nearly all the publications received by our churches are for our own members. As a result, we fail to nurture an environment in which all members constantly and systematically participate in reaching the world through literature.

We must not confuse the functions of the literature evangelist with what church members should be doing. Though literature evangelists mostly sell, it can be more than that. They can lend or give away materials. And here is where our churches should promote regular programs that encourage their members to participate in proclaiming the sealing message.

Fortunately, the problem is nearing a solution. In 2010 church members in the South American Division distributed 30 million magazines plus a book on the Sabbath in a project called Hope Impact 2010.[15] In addition, as mentioned in chapter 4, the General Conference has launched a plan to distribute 200 million copies of *The Great Controversy through the membership. And the idea is to carry this project throughout the world.*

Things are changing for the better. Many are waking up to realize that if we really want to reach the world and finish the mission of preaching to every creature, then we must undertake the method envisioned by Ellen G. White and commanded by God.[16] And to help matters along, the church must learn what colportage—to use the original term—really means.

Origin of the word "colporteur"

Etymologically the word "colporteur" derives from old French. It is a compound word made of up "col," which in French means "the neck of the coat or shirt" (or "cou," a person's neck), and "porteur," which in French means "bearer" or "carrier."[17] It came to be used for peddlers of religious books.

The church adopted the word for our publications program, an allusion to the activity carried on by the Waldenses in the twelfth century. Adventists regarded them as conducting a work similar to what the church must now do. The Waldenses specialized in copying portions of the Scriptures, which they then gave away to certain people, and they carried them in hidden bags hanging from their necks.[18]

Therefore the word "colporteur" became a technical term to identify those whose job was to spread the gospel through printed means similar to what the Waldenses did. I want to underscore that it was not launched for commercial purposes, neither among Waldenses in the twelfth century nor later by Adventists in the nineteenth century.

In the case of the Waldenses, according to Nicolás Chaij, "an inquisitor describes them traveling from town to town selling wares with which to get into the homes. He explains that they sold jewelry, rings, bonnets, fabrics, veils, and other finery. If asked whether they carried any other finery, they would reply, 'Yes, we carry jewels finer than these. If you promise not to turn us in, we will show them to you.' After getting a proper assurance, the colporteurs would say, '*We have a precious stone so brilliant that its light allows one to contemplate God; and so radiant, that it ignites love for God in the heart of its possessor. We are using figurative language, yet we are telling you the very truth.*'

"They would then pull out a portion of the Bible from under their coats, and, after reading it, would explain it and would sell to thirsty souls the living water. Thus did they sow the precious seed that sprouted, grew, and bore precious fruit. . . . Thus, the courageous Waldensian colporteurs gave birth to this missionary method, sowing God's invincible Word, and prepared the way for the Reformation, which has not yet run its course, but will continue until the end of time."[19]

And that was the beginning of literature evangelism. On the other hand, when Ellen G. White had a vision in 1848 calling Adventists to print, the emphasis was the *proclamation of the sealing message.* Therefore, those who sell our literature today must bear in mind that they are involved in *a prophetic vocation.* Their aim and objective is to spread truth that lights the paths of many. Now, what exactly does that mean?

Waldenses of the third millennium

Many restrict or abandon literature evangelism because of misunderstanding. Some in the church associate it with just another way to make a living. But it is much more than selling books door to door. It helps to set the world stage for the proclamation of the loud cry in Holy Spirit power that will gather into the heavenly garner much golden grain.

That is why we must abandon a commercial mind-set. While giving a family a message-bearing book might not strictly be colporteuring, it is fulfilling its mission, which means that distributed books do not need to be sold to fall under the label of literature evangelism.

If every church member understood this, many more would become Waldenses of the third millennium. And the church is getting ready to do just that. Many are asking for thousands of books to use in sharing our message. Those with means can sponsor thousands of books and, in some cases, even give a stipend for distributors to reach neighborhoods, towns, or even entire cities.

So what does it mean to colporteur in modern times?

Colporteuring: a working definition

If we look at what the Bible and Ellen G. White have to say, we arrive at the following: Colporteuring (literature evangelism) is to bear the three angels' messages in written form to those not of our faith and to those who know not the gospel through books, magazines, or tracts, either lent, sold, or given away.

Bible and Ellen G. White basis for the definition

To colporteur is to bear. We cannot wait for the people to come to us. They do not know who we are, and rarely do they seek us out on their own initiative. How many know that God has entrusted Seventh-day Adventists with the task of giving the world the last solemn, divine warning? How many know that the Adventist Church has a whole arsenal of literature containing truth for our time? Very few do. But Jesus makes no mistake, and He knew what He was doing when He gave the command to go to the ends of the earth (see Matt. 28:19; Acts 1:8).

The third angel's message. The message we share must be that of the three angels. After the disappointment of 1844 we were instructed to prophesy again (see Rev. 10:11). Of course, the proclamation of the message of the third angel started back there. And it was the message not only of the "everlasting gospel" but also specifically that the "hour of judgment is come" (Rev. 14:6, 7). And since to stand in the judgment means to come under the scrutiny of God's law (Rom. 2:12), the guidepost to keep from straying is contained in the third angel's message (Rev. 14:9-12). The second angel helps us to see that "Babylon is fallen" (verse 8), and the angel of Revelation 18 reiterates the warning and extends an invitation to come out of her. That is the work of the church.

If our priorities do not include leaving with people books containing this truth, then we are giving the world only refined spiritual flour, one that contains none of the essential ingredients necessary to make strong believers who will triumph in the soon-coming crisis. Paradoxically, we can provide "nutrition" to families through our health message, yet leave them unfamiliar with the message of the third angel.

In written form. This is in keeping with the witnessing and preaching models ordained by God since ancient times. The Lord ordered Moses to write (Deut. 27:3; 31:19; Ex. 24:4), as He did Jeremiah (Jer. 36:2) and John (Rev. 1:11, 19). And God, by giving this command once more in 1848, proposes to continue using the method that has worked so well in the past. Or dare we imagine that God, called the Only Wise, would use anything but the very best methods in carrying out His grand designs?

Those not of our faith. It implies that other religions and denominations need the message we have. Ellen White tells us that "the professed Christian churches are not converting the world."[20] Some might assume that the people in those churches will refuse to hear the message, but the prophecy calls us to take the gospel to those in Babylon. God has children in those churches, and we must invite them to join us. In fact, the message of the second angel is precisely that (Rev. 14:8).

Know not the gospel. The Lord "will have all men to be saved, and to come unto the knowledge of the truth" (1 Tim. 2:4), yet multitudes today know nothing of the gospel. God's command to prophesy includes "every creature" (Mark 16:15), and literature plays a crucial part in reaching them.

John declares that the great object of the printed page is for people to be saved (John 20:30, 31), and Luke tells us that the purpose of the written ministry is for people to know the truth with a "perfect understanding (Luke 1:1-4).

Through books, magazines, or tracts. It goes without saying but still bears emphasizing that such books, magazines, and tracts must necessarily contain a message that people cannot get anywhere else. Books on health and family life, though important in themselves, are not what the people need the most. What they require are publications that contain the decisive truths, and yet the health message is part of the third angel's message. Before the world confronts the results of continued transgression of the moral law, we must warn people about the consequences of the laws governing our physical selves, laws inscribed in our very being (Rev. 14:9; Gen. 2:7).

At the same time, books bearing on our families' well-being have to do with the message of the third Elijah. Malachi tells us that before "the coming of the great and dreadful day of the Lord" Elijah shall "turn the heart of the fathers to the children, and the heart of the children to their fathers" (Mal. 4:5, 6).

Therefore the literature evangelist who takes the whole message to the people is fulfilling this prophecy. A balance between books dealing with health and family and those containing the last warning truths for our world forms the comprehensive message that God has ordained for the good of the masses. In other words, the wares of literature evangelists constitute the *most complete missionary message* in compact form.

I believe that of all the ministries in our church, only the literature evangelist offers a truly comprehensive presentation. It includes not only the testing truths for our time, but also gives the world what it needs to remedy its physical and mental maladies. As such, the work of the literature evangelist is truly a superior one. We should appreciate them better for this.

Even so, Ellen White reminds us, "We are now altogether too near the close of this earth's history to keep before the attention of the people a class of books which do not contain the message which our people need."[21] Our mission *will not be complete* unless and until we combine books on health and books on practical godliness with those bearing the testing truths for our time. We must work intelligently, making decided efforts "to carry our important religious books to the people."[22]

Thus far we have seen that we can present our message through books, magazines, and tracts, but what are the biblical reasons for doing that? If we examine the message God gave to the churches, we find the following:

Books. The Lord told John, "What thou seest, write in a book, and send it unto the seven churches which are in Asia" (Rev. 1:11). Similarly He directed Jeremiah to "take a scroll and write on it" (Jer. 36:2, NIV).

Books are at the heart of God's plan to give the world the knowledge necessary for salvation. Ellen White wrote that *"it is wrong to leave lying on the shelves the large works* that the Lord has revealed should be put into the hands of the people, and to push so vigorously, in the place of these, the sale of small books."[23] More comprehensive books have their own place in the plan of salvation.

Magazines. Imagine getting a letter spanning 15 chapters, totaling 23 pages. You might think of it as being not a letter, but a magazine. But that's what the early churches received from Paul, for example. The letters to the Romans and Corinthians teach us an important lesson: Though the Bible as a whole presents God's truth for humanity, it is everywhere presented in small bites or pieces. Why?

Ellen White explains: "It will be difficult for some minds to fathom our most difficult works, and a simpler way of putting the truth will reach them more readily." And she adds that "pamphlets that dwell upon Bible lessons . . . need attention in the canvassing work, for they are as little wedges that open the way for larger works."[24]

From this perspective magazines, too, have their place in the great plan of salvation. First, because they are just what certain minds will need. Second, because they prepare the way for our larger volumes. Finally, because they outline things in a quickly comprehended way vital for today's fast-paced lifestyles, especially when we are told that the "final movements will be rapid ones."[25]

Tracts. Distributing tracts and pamphlets is also literature evangelism, though it may be difficult for many in the church to accept this. But, for example, the Third Epistle of John the apostle or Jude's letter could easily fit in a tract-sized format—yet they have their place in the sacred canon.

"Numberless words need not be put upon paper to justify what speaks for itself and shines in its clearness. Truth is straight, plain, clear, and stands out boldly in its own defense; but it is not so with error. It is so winding and twisting that it needs a multitude of words to explain it in its crooked form."[26]

In the final crisis, the more direct the message, the better.

Lent, sold, or given away

This expression may seem unfamiliar to many, especially since we usually consider literature evangelism primarily as "selling." Historically, however, neither the Waldenses nor the church pioneers emphasized selling. Everything revolved around preaching the gospel in as rapid and efficient a way as possible. The idea of selling our publications was a later development, a result of the maturing of our publishing program. Yet even there the idea of selling literature has a scriptural basis, as we will see.

Lent: This idea is 100 percent biblical. As Paul wrote "And when this epistle is read among you, cause that it be read also in the church of the Laodiceans; and that ye likewise read the epistle from Laodicea" (Col. 4:16). This is what theologians call "Paul's circulating letters."

Can we grasp what would happen if every single person in the church determined to lend one book per month to those not familiar with the gospel? We're talking millions of homes reached.

"Think of how great a work can be done if a large number of believers will unite in an effort to place before the people, by the circulation of these books, the light that the Lord has said should be given them."[27]

It, of course, applies with equal force to the selling and giving away of our materials.

Sold: Books and Bibles come with a production cost, and someone must pay for it. As Jesus said: "The labourer is worthy of his hire" (Luke 10:7), and He commanded "that they which preach the gospel should live of the gospel" (1 Cor. 9:14). Jesus casts Himself as a door-to-door salesperson in the closing scenes of earth's history, counseling His hearers to buy from Him (Rev. 3:18-20). Despite such vivid imagery, selling should never become an end in itself.

"If our canvassers are controlled by the spirit of financial gain, if they circulate the book upon which they can make the most money, to the neglect of others that the people need, I ask, In what sense is theirs a missionary work?"[28]

The problem is not in earning a good income but rather when the income itself starts becoming the primary motivation.

Given away: Biblical counsel declares, *"Buy the truth, and sell it not"* (Prov. 23:23). We must be willing to pay any price to know the truth but never to part with it at any cost. But is this the same as selfishly hoarding it? The Bible counsels us to "deal thy bread to the hungry" (Isa. 58:7). Therefore the truest interpretation of the Word is not that our literature cannot be sold, but rather never to part with the principles of righteousness. Instead, we are to make the truth available to as many as will respond. We must give away the truth—at any price.

Conclusion

Literature evangelism is taking the third angel's message in written form to those not of our faith, and to those unfamiliar with the gospel message. It can be through books, magabooks, magazines, or tracts, whether lent, sold, or given away.

As a church we have a great work ahead of us. Our mission encompasses a whole world. It is for this reason that "God calls for workers from every church among us to enter His service as canvasser evangelists. . . . If the members will do His will, if they will strive to impart the light to those in darkness, He will greatly bless their efforts. . . . Through its faithful ministrations, *a multitude that no man can number will become children of God, fitted for the everlasting glory.*"[29]

Then the Lord presents a challenge: "Let every Seventh-day Adventist ask himself, 'What can I do to proclaim the third angel's message?' Christ came to this world to give this message to His servant to give to the churches. It is to be proclaimed to every nation, kindred, tongue, and people. How are we to give it? The *distribution of our literature is one means by which the message is to be proclaimed. Let every believer scatter broadcast tracts and leaflets and books containing the message for this time.*"[30]

General Conference president Ted N. C. Wilson recently said, "My vision for the publishing ministries sector . . . includes a deep desire that house-to-house ministry will continue as a major part of each literature evangelist's program, [and that] many thousands of members will join in circulating the missionary book of the year."[31]

Pastor Alejandro Bullón observes that "if every church member would distribute our publications wherever they live, the gospel would have been preached with greater efficiency and timeliness."[32] So if you are a full-time literature evangelist, understand that it is no ordinary occupation. It is in fact a work every bit as important as that of the ordained minister, one that most closely approaches the current needs in our world as well as those we are soon to face.

"Why should not every member of the church be as deeply interested in sending forth publications that will elevate the minds of the people, and bring the truth directly before them? These papers and tracts are for the light of the world, and have often been instrumental in converting souls."[33] Furthermore, "there is much to be done to advance the work of God. I have been instructed that the canvassing work is to be revived, and that it is to be carried forward with increasing success."[34]

We are certainly seeing a revival of the publishing ministry within the church, and it is starting to be noticed. For example, according to a report by Tercio Márques, a single church in São Paulo, Brazil, has distributed more than 215,000 copies of *The Great Hope*.[35] Yet we must view it only as the beginning of what the Lord would have us do at this time. Moreover we can truly say that God's Spirit is now stirring many hearts in the church to undertake a great work. Miracles are being seen. Wouldn't you like to form a part of this great awakening?

Is the Lord calling on you, dear reader? You can reach members of your family who today do not know the gospel. They may be far away, but a book can touch them no matter where they are. What about your friends and neighbors? If you knew they would never hear the truth unless you gave it to them, wouldn't you start today?

Remember that a book preaches truth no matter where its location, and the church has a moral obligation to present truth in written form.

Anyone can be a part of the publishing ministry! It simply involves distributing the message of the sealing in written form with the sole objective of saving "the great multitude." Never forget that the only way of saving the world from the deadly delusions of the time of the end is *by sealing it. All who are not sealed will receive the mark of the beast and the seven last plagues. As such, who will be the last messenger of mercy to a world racing to its ruin? It could be you! It could be a book you give away. Will you take up the challenge?*

---

[1] E. G. White, *Christian Service*, p. 253. (Italics supplied.)

[2] G. Verwer, *Literature Evangelism*, p. 1.

[3] Dale E. Galusha, "Transforming the Ordinary: A Most Important Work," *The Literature Evangelist,* October-December 2009, p. 3, http://publishing.gc.adventist.org/files/pdf/LEMIssue689.pdf.

[4] E. G. White, *Christian Service*, p. 196. (Italics supplied.)

[5] D. Eastman, *Beyond Imagination*, p. 13.

[6] G. R. Knight, *Organizing to Beat the Devil*, p. 8. (Italics supplied.)

[7] G. Zaid, *So Many Books*, p. 83.

[8] See John Williamson Tyler, *Beautiful Story of the Bible in Simple Language Containing Nearly Three Hundred Stories From the Holy Book* (Marietta, Ohio: S. A. Mulikin Co., 1919).

[9] *The Seventh-day Adventist Bible Commentary,* Ellen G. White Comments, vol. 3, p. 1134. (Italics supplied.)

[10] Ellen G. White, *Christian Experience and Teachings of Ellen G. White* (Mountain View, Calif.: Pacific Press Pub. Assn., 1922), p. 225.

[11] Ellen G. White, *Life Sketches of Ellen G. White* (Mountain View, Calif.: Pacific Press Pub. Assn., 1915), p. 211. (Italics supplied.)

[12] *Ibid.,* p. 217. (Italics supplied.)

[13] See http://en.wikipedia.org/wiki/Jehovah%27s_Witness_publications#cite_note-9.

[14] E. G. White, *Colporteur Ministry,* p. 151.

[15] Almir Marroni, "Ten Million Contacts per Year," *The Literature Evangelist,* April-September 2010, p. 18.

[16] E. G. White, *Colporteur Ministry,* p. 5.

[17] Benjamín Riffel, *Éxito sin Límites* [*Success Without Limits*] (Puebla, México: Publicaciones Interamericanas, 1983), p. 21.

[18] See chapter 4, "The Waldenses," in E. G. White, *The Great Controversy.*

[19] Nicolás Chaij, *El Colportor de Éxito* [*The Successful Colporteur*] (Bogotá: Asociación Publicadora Interamericana, 1994), p. 23.

[20] E. G. White, *Colporteur to Ministry,* p. 2.

[21] *Ibid.,* p. 141.

[22] *Ibid.*

[23] *Ibid.* (Italics supplied.)

[24] *Ibid.,* p. 140.

[25] E. G. White, *Last Day Events,* p. 11.

[26] E. G. White, *Early Writings,* p. 96.

[27] E. G. White, *Colporteur Ministry,* p. 22.

[28] *Ibid.,* p. 97.

[29] *Ibid.,* p. 20. (Italics supplied.)

[30] Ellen G. White, *The Publishing Ministry* (Washington, D.C.: Review and Herald Pub. Assn., 1983), p. 349. (Italics supplied.)

[31] Ted N. C. Wilson, "A Personal Letter From Our World Church President."

[32] A. Bullón, *Sharing Jesus Is Everything,* p. 124.

[33] E. G. White, *Christian Service,* p. 146.

[34] E. G. White, *Colporteur Ministry,* p. 17.

[35] http://greatcontroversyproject.adventist.org/newsletter.html; newsletter, Feb. 6, 2012.